Gerry Brown
Making a Difference

Gerry Brown

Making a Difference

Leadership, Change and Giving Back the Independent
Director Way

DE GRUYTER

ISBN 978-3-11-070607-9
e-ISBN (PDF) 978-3-11-070612-3
e-ISBN (EPUB) 978-3-11-070622-2

Library of Congress Control Number: 2020945833

Bibliographic information published by the Deutsche Nationalbibliothek
The Deutsche Nationalbibliothek lists this publication in the Deutsche Nationalbibliografie;
detailed bibliographic data are available on the Internet at http://dnb.dnb.de.

© 2021 Walter de Gruyter GmbH, Berlin/Boston
Cover image: Mario and Aurora Brown
Typesetting: Integra Software Services Pvt. Ltd.
Printing and binding: CPI books GmbH, Leck

www.degruyter.com

Advance praise for *Making a Difference*

In the wake of the Covid pandemic, there is a critical need for a generous sharing of energy and expertise as we all seek to understand how we can work in the 'new normal'. For those with energy, valuable skills and appropriate expertise, volunteering as an independent director is an effective way of giving for the collective good. In this book, Gerry Brown sets out the role of independent directors: how talented and informed volunteers can contribute as counsellors, guides and mentors in helping organisations steer strategy, manage risk, ensure accountability and deliver to stakeholders. In his eloquent, succinct and pragmatic style, Gerry explains the why, what and how. Why become an independent director? What's involved? What are the challenges and opportunities? How to choose and approach organisations? Why me? What does it take? There is no better time, or more important time, to step forward and share our energy, expertise and wisdom to help organisations, businesses and society move forward in the new world.

– Professor Malcolm Kirkup
Pro Vice Chancellor, University of Westminster
Head, Westminster Business School

If you are considering becoming an independent director (or governor) of a business, charity, educational establishment, sports body or similar, then Gerry Brown's book is an essential read. Drawing on his own extensive experience and through interviews with a variety of successful IDs, he explains why there is a need for more diverse boards which can provide sound governance in today's complex and fast moving world. Equally for the experienced chair or board member, this book serves as an outstanding guide to best practice governance.

In my role as the Further Education Commissioner for England I have learned how important good governance is, both within colleges and elsewhere in business, charities and beyond. The best boards that I have encountered always include a diverse range of independent directors, an open culture led by the chair, and a willingness to both support and challenge the executive. Gerry Brown's excellent book is the perfect guide for anyone considering joining a governing body as an independent director, as well as being a best practice guide for existing chairs and IDs. As organisations rebuild after the impact of the pandemic, there has never been a more important time to provide good governance.

– Richard Atkins, Further Education Commissioner,
Council Member, The University of Exeter

https://doi.org/10.1515/9783110706123-202

Gerry Brown is a passionate advocate of board room diversity.

Not only that, he challenges us all to take on one of these roles, and see it as a means to make a much wider contribution to society; a way of growing our life experience. He is very persuasive, with many real world examples.

But this is a book full of realism as well. Rightly he points out that no one is going to be appointed first time as an FT-100 non-executive. But your contribution will be fulfilling not just to you, but to society more widely. It can be the first rung on a ladder to bigger things.

The book is also practical. It advises those entering this world, at whatever level, how to approach your first meeting and how to grow in the role. It makes it clear that the job can involve difficult decisions – whether to fire the chairman or the CEO could be one of them.

One thing is clear, with all the challenges that we face, we need a breath of fresh air in our board rooms whether local or national, charity or business. That diverse talent is out there. Gerry Brown's strong advocacy is a means of making it happen.

– Lord Robin Teverson, former Member of the European Parliament

To my brother Ben, who has been an inspiration to everyone through his charitable work for the mentally handicapped despite his own illness. He is a living example of Making a Difference.

Acknowledgements

My thanks go to many people.

To Teena Lyons for helping to translate my thoughts and ideas into a manuscript, including interviewing all of the contributors.

To Jeff Scott for helping with the structure of the book and for being a very professional publicist.

To Marilyn Livingstone for preparing the index.

To my son Mario and granddaughter Aurora for producing a wonderful book cover.

To daughters Cayetana and Francisca for their work in organising the book launch.

To Edmee for her help with the book launch.

To all of those who agreed to contribute by being interviewed, including Dipti Amin, Richard Atkins, Helen Baker, Ruth Cairnie, Jane Chafer, Mike Clancy, Patrick Dunne, Janie Frampton, Jonathan Hurst, Liz Johnson, Michelle Leavesley, Richard Sargeant, Sir Peter Thompson, Sarah Turvill, and Devyani Vaishampayan.

To those who have proofread the manuscript and reviewed it, including Peter Weston, David Parfett, Morgen Witzel, and Dr. Roger Barker.

To those who have reviewed the book, including Lord Teverson, Professor Malcolm Kirkup, Richard Atkins, Charlotte Valeur, and Chris Hopson.

https://doi.org/10.1515/9783110706123-203

Contents

About the author

Gerry Brown is currently chairman of Novaquest Capital Management, a private equity firm focussed on life sciences and of GBrown Associates Ltd., a family company providing consultancy services.

He was an independent director of Quintiles, the world's largest clinical research organisation. He was chairman of Biocompatibles International PLC, a medical devices company, and of NFT Ltd., a private equity backed MBO from Northern Foods. He was senior independent director of Keller PLC, a leading global construction services company, and of Forth Ports PLC, a ports and property company. He represented 3i on the board of Vantec Corporation, an MBO from Nissan in Japan until the extremely successful exit. He was chairman of Upol Ltd., a director of CH Jones Ltd., a non-executive director of Michael Gerson Ltd., and of Datrontech PLC, an international distributor of computer products.

Prior to his career as a chairman/independent director, Gerry was for many years an international senior business executive working in supply chain management, covering a variety of market sectors. He served as operations director of Exel PLC (now DHL), was a board member of TDG PLC and was chairman of Europe for Tibbett and Britten PLC. He is a fellow of the Institute of Directors and a fellow of the Chartered Institute of Logistics. He is a member of the Council of Exeter University and chair of the Audit Committee and of the Fundraising Board. He is an associate of Criticaleye and mentors CEOs, and is the author of *The Independent Director* and lead author of *The Independent Director in Society*.

Gerry is a visiting fellow at Henley Business School and is a member of the Advisory Board on Corporate Governance of The Institute of Directors.

https://doi.org/10.1515/9783110706123-205

Introduction

Diversification is strength. The reality is, if you want positive change, and you want your organisation, or charity, or sport, or governing body, whatever it is, to best serve its community, then your board needs to truly represent the community it is trying to serve.

Liz Johnson, Board Member, Disability Sport Wales

In the spring of 2020, when the UK joined much of the rest of the world in the coronavirus (Covid-19) lockdown, more than one million people stepped forward to volunteer within a matter of days. The NHS volunteer scheme saw 750,000 register on a phone app, which was three times the level expected, while volunteer centres registered a further 250,000 who were eager to help. Meanwhile, hundreds of thousands of people quietly stepped up in their own ways, making DIY PPE equipment for health workers, delivering food to the elderly and vulnerable or setting up informal 'good neighbour' networks. We have not seen a mobilisation of volunteers on this scale since the Second World War, when more than one million registered with the Royal Voluntary Society to help with the evacuation of children from cities devastated by the Blitz.

While the individual motivations to help might have varied, there is no doubt at all that there was one dominant impulse: to make a difference.

The surge in the desire to help one another is not a unique phenomenon. Granted, social volunteering increases hugely at a time of national stress and tension, but it is something that is ever-present in British society. Prior to the pandemic, millions of people a year were donating money, volunteering their time and helping out in their community every single day. Elsewhere, when they were able to, countless citizens marched on the streets in a bid to make their voices heard, highlighting their concerns over the climate emergency, gender inequality, animal rights and other very worthwhile causes.

At the time of writing this book, we are in search of the 'new normal'. I suspect that by the time this is published, we will still be in a similar situation. While there is no doubt that we face many uncertainties in the near future, my hope is that this collective spirit which has seen so many people helping one another will endure. There is, I believe, more of a need than ever for people to help each other. Yes, 2020 has been tough, but it would be wrong to waste the unity, cohesiveness and sheer energy to help others that the global health emergency provoked. We have an opportunity here to help change society for the better and to make a real, lasting and tangible difference to the cause/s and community groups we feel most strongly about. And what is one of the most effective ways to do this at the highest level? Become an independent director and effect change from within.

Independent directors (IDs) aren't just found in the boardrooms of blue chip companies. They play a vital role in governing a wide range of organisations from the NHS, to charities, to sporting bodies, to educational establishments and

https://doi.org/10.1515/9783110706123-206

beyond. This is the opportunity to change the direction, trajectory and understanding of corporate social responsibility initiatives for the businesses, charities and health and social groups that serve our communities in the post–Covid-19 age. Now more than ever, these organisations will be relying on talented and informed volunteers to ensure their campaigns reach the wider world and serve the communities that are so in need of assistance. Independent directors not only steer and develop strategy while managing risk, but they are also the key to ensuring accountability and making sure the aims of these organisations are being met. They are the people who steadfastly ensure that all stakeholders are properly served, be it employees, customers or society at large, rather than simply those with a direct financial interest. They are the real long-term custodians of organisations.

IDs act as a counsellor, guide and mentor to others on boards and management committees, while also overseeing compliance with relevant laws and regulations. Equally important, IDs stand back and take in the optics from an outsider's point of view, ensuring an organisation is governed in a moral way. If they see what they perceive to be a failure of governance, it is their job to speak out and steer the organisation in a better direction.

When I first started writing this book, in the days before anyone had heard of Covid-19, my motivation was that there were too many boards that were not nearly as effective as they might be. Over the years, there have been just too many governance scandals which proved that the system of checks and balances that should have been performed by independent directors was not working as well as it should – in some cases, not even close. Stories have broken with alarming frequency about catastrophic failures in both public and private organisations, even after numerous codes have been put in place to prevent this from happening. When boards fall short, the vital work of any organisation is curtailed, or, in the worst-case scenario, stopped altogether.

There is now a growing body of evidence that shows that the boards that operate most effectively are the ones that are most diverse. The result is diversity of thought, better decision-making and an improved outcome for all. Unfortunately, for too long, boardrooms and management committees have overwhelmingly been filled with people who look largely the same. To coin a phrase, they are largely male, pale and stale.

Blame for any inefficiencies can't just be laid at the door of boards. Reports indicate that while many institutions recognise the need for a broader base on their management committees, many are struggling to find willing recruits. Recruitment consultancies report returning to the same people to fish from the same pool time and again. Why? Because no one else is putting themselves forward.

Boardrooms are crying out for diverse, committed and engaged independent directors – not just the boards of big corporations, either. The reason this book focusses on positions on boards that are mainly outside the corporate arena –

whether they are health trusts, charities, sporting organisations, universities or community groups – is because, post-pandemic, these organisations are under more pressure than ever before to perform well, with considerably less money to do so. After years of austerity and cuts in public services, followed by the devastation of Covid-19, those organisations that have not collapsed altogether are crumbling under the strain. The enormous increase in the national debt will make these challenges even greater. We all have a responsibility to do all we can to help.

It is my personal goal to vastly increase the number of people who are willing to step up and become independent directors. It is only by attracting this wider group of talented and committed IDs who can contribute so much more that we will be able to effect some real, positive change. My aim with this book is to fully explain what being an independent director entails, why your skills are in big demand and how it is possible for you to truly make a difference.

I am heartened by the fact that my quest to grow the ranks of IDs is not starting from nothing. Over and above the recent surge in Covid-19 volunteers, there have already been ample signs of a groundswell of interest in stepping up to tackle social and environmental problems. There has been a huge drive particularly by millennials to volunteer and make a difference. The so-called Generation Z, who have no faith in the political system or in the abilities or will of politicians to effect change, have been stepping up for a good while now and have been offering to do the job themselves. In fact, many won't even consider a full-time job unless there is some opportunity to contribute in some way to solving wider problems in the community around them. In more prosperous times, there was an increased willingness by employers to give their employees paid time off to do something that makes a difference. Why? Because pride is a powerful motivator. The feeling that what you do is worthwhile drives exceptional service, continued innovation and commitment, which of course benefits the main employer. Corporations know that encouraging their team to give a little back to society is not just a tick in the box for Corporate Social Responsibility – it brings with it the advantages of increased productivity, innovation and staff retention. Plus, it affords any company the opportunity to bring about a positive change on a mass scale by significantly impacting wider society and changing people's lives for the better.

Over the period of writing this book, the world changed completely. Organisations everywhere are under more pressure than ever as they go through the great changes and adjustments that are required following the pandemic and the resultant devastating economic slowdown. While the crisis has changed so much for everyone, it is my hope that we can harness some of that community spirit and maintain the deeply felt desire to help others. I would be delighted if many of the million plus volunteers turned their attention to the potential of becoming an independent director. There are many people who have lost their jobs in 2020, or who experienced a prolonged period of furlough. These people will be looking for ways to stay active in the workplace. Others will still be working, but will see the value of using some of their skills and expertise to help people in the community who have not been so fortunate. Whatever the motivation, there is a powerful argument in favour of harnessing this sentiment to encourage more people to take on independent director roles, which will benefit everyone.

For too long, independent directors have been seen as decorative, as an appendage rather than a key feature and a way to drive meaningful change across business, public policy and our communities. With the onset of the Covid-19 crisis comes the need for original thought-leadership that can make a real difference as Britain rebuilds towards a brighter, more collaborative future. There is a real opportunity here to create a new generation of fully committed, knowledgeable IDs with the passion to do the right thing, which is exactly what is needed to help boards function properly.

In order to thoroughly explain everything that is involved and answer any questions that you may have, I have included numerous examples of good practice, instances where I believe that IDs have been worth their weight in gold and have demonstrated so. To help me in this task, I have interviewed a number of IDs who have made a positive difference for their organisations, and their stories form a very important and interesting part of this book. These luminaries are drawn from backgrounds in business, education, charity, sport and health, and all have a wealth of experience of the qualities an effective ID requires, as well as the challenges they might face. I have found their contributions invaluable and I am sure you will too.

I have been careful to document the challenges involved. Becoming an ID is not always the easy option. There are a number of personal attributes that are key, such as a clear need to be able to manage and influence people. Often, this means challenging some powerful voices in the boardroom, which is not always an easy thing to do when big personalities are involved. I have described some of the skills and techniques that will help in this endeavour in this book. My view is that these challenges should be viewed as a positive, since understanding and learning to deal with them are important parts of career and personal development, which will most likely be useful elsewhere in your working life, not to mention interesting to learn.

I don't deny that at times it will be hard work, but doing anything worthwhile is never easy. Certainly, we are a long way from the days where an ID can get away with turning up at meetings after a cursory glance at board papers beforehand, then leaving after making a few pithy observations. And rightly so. In today's highly connected world, there is an expectation that IDs are fully appraised of all the issues impacting the boards they serve on a real-time basis. Each of the contributors I spoke with mentioned 'commitment' on more than one occasion. It is for this very reason that I suggest that if you choose to pursue any independent directorships, it has to be concerned with something you are passionate about.

As a housekeeping point, I would like to point out that I have mainly used the term *independent director*, or ID, throughout this book, even though there are other terms used for the same position. The most common alternative in the corporate world is *non-executive director*, or NED, while *trustee*, *governor* or *board member* are used elsewhere in public or in non-profit positions. I've used the term ID for consistency, but also to emphasise the independence of the role and to separate them from the paid executives. IDs have an engaged stewardship role which is to ensure that companies are managed in the best interest of all stakeholders, not just shareholders. I have also used the terms *boards* and *management committees* interchangeably. The terms for these governing bodies do vary by sector.

My strong wish is that this book will go a long way toward persuading you that there is an opportunity to make a difference and to convince you to put yourself forward. I have already seen many very important breakthroughs through my own work coaching and assisting the next generation of IDs through organisations such as Criticaleye and the *Financial Times*. These experiences prompted me to write this book because I am now more convinced than ever that a more diverse, active board presence will have a huge impact on the future direction of organisations in the public and private sectors. It really is possible to make a significant difference as an ID. At the same time, there are many personal benefits such as the opportunity to experience different challenges, learn a great deal and work alongside people in different organisations and cultures.

However hard it is out there right now, as we adapt to the new normal, there are also numerous opportunities to help our society to change for the better. Volunteering and bringing the community back to the core of what we are about is what sustains us. Becoming an ID is the right way to rise to the challenge and use your skills to address the issues you care most deeply about.

Here's how.

Chapter 1
Giving back is the best way forward

The decision to make a difference often stems from a deep-seated desire to right a wrong. People want to do their bit to improve something in society that is just not right, however small or incidental that action might seem. Frequently though, what seems like the smallest action to make a change can escalate into something very significant indeed. This is certainly the case with Patrick Dunne.

Take a look at Patrick's LinkedIn page today and you will see a long list of board successes spanning Europe, Asia and North America, as well as details of an impressive career as a serial social entrepreneur. He spent nine years as the chair of Leap, an organisation that helps some of our most challenged young people manage conflict more easily. He also chaired the EY Foundation, which also helps disadvantaged youth; ESSA, a start-up focussed on transforming education and career prospects in Sub-Saharan Africa; and Boardelta, a consultancy focussed on making a difference to boards. His executive roles include 26 years at 3i, the international private equity and venture capital firm. What makes this all the more remarkable is that Patrick did not start out with the proverbial silver spoon in his mouth. This is, according to Patrick, just why he was compelled to follow the path he has and worked so diligently to put back in as much as he has been able to.

His story began with a childhood in a 'difficult part' of Liverpool and he freely admits there were a fair number of challenges growing up. Even so, his mother instilled a strong ethic of generosity into the family.

'In her view, there was always someone who was worse off than we were,' Patrick said. 'It was our duty to help.'

This philosophy struck a deep note with Patrick who, against the odds, managed to get a place at university and then a well-paid job. He began volunteering when at school with residential care company Leonard Cheshire, alongside numerous part-time jobs to make ends meet. As his career progressed, he continued to volunteer, mostly through Rotaract. He eventually joined 3i after completing an MBA and began to wonder if he could do more. Specifically, he started to question how he could use all the skills he had gained in the pursuit of building businesses, and put them to work building charities. His thoughts kept coming back to his own experience. Although mildly dyslexic, after a tricky start, Patrick had done well at school. It was the classic scenario: an inspirational teacher spotted his potential, in this case in maths, and encouraged him to build upon his skills. There were, Patrick decided, clear signposts from his story that might be able to help him find a way to support and inspire other disadvantaged young people to realise their own potential through education.

By lucky coincidence, as Patrick was formulating his thoughts, he was given the opportunity to become responsible for 3i's charity budget. He felt the spending wasn't

https://doi.org/10.1515/9783110706123-001

focussed and that there was an opportunity to have a lot more impact. He persuaded the 3i board to focus the activity on supporting young disadvantaged people through education.

'It was about applying venture capital techniques to increase social impact,' he says. 'I wanted to do more than giving a little bit of money to a lot of different causes and then forgetting about it.'

The strategy proved to be successful and soon led to a new opportunity to make a difference for young people. By this stage, Patrick had done a great deal of training around board development. This was primarily to help him be more effective when working with 3i's clients, but the unexpected consequence was that a number of charitable boards came knocking. Could Patrick help them? Naturally, the one offer that Patrick was particularly attracted to was Leap, because of its focus on helping young people. It was not the obvious choice though – at the time, the charity was quite small and didn't even have a website. Once again, Patrick followed his business strategy of going all-in to make a big impact, and very soon after, he saw results.

Patrick's next foray into making a difference struck right into the heart of the motivations that had been generated from his own upbringing. He received an approach from an academic at Warwick University who told him that applications for maths degrees had dried up from in and around Coventry. A little digging revealed that a number of schools had dropped further maths A' Levels from the Curriculum, thanks to budgets cuts. Further maths is a prerequisite for a place on the Warwick University maths degree. Additional research into schools further afield revealed the same thing. Most poignantly, the school in Liverpool, where Patrick had studied and excelled at maths, could no longer afford to offer the further maths course either.

The Warwick University academic who alerted Patrick to the issue only wanted an investment of just £5000 to set up a scheme that would train teachers in the further maths curriculum. Patrick got involved and the initiative became a big success. In fact, it evolved into the Further Maths Network, a hugely successful nationwide scheme.

Once again, Patrick started to think about the crossover between his day job and his charitable work. Were there lessons from the maths network success story that could be used to help other people? In his 3i role, whenever something worked well, he'd always worked on ways of developing it elsewhere by, say, launching a similar version in another country, or format. Could the same be done with the further maths model? The thought process led to volunteers who had pioneered the scheme in Coventry being sent to Africa to teach kids from even less privileged backgrounds. Again, it has been a huge success. Starting in Johannesburg, South Africa, the scheme has now expanded into Tanzania and Kenya. More than 750,000 kids have benefited from the training, which has been shown to improve maths results by 30%.

'I'm incredibly lucky that there was this crossover with the role at 3i, focusing on boards and portfolio companies,' Patrick says. 'These were skills that I could transfer to tackle the stuff that needs tackling. It enabled me to step up and make a real difference.'

—

Right now, it is still impossible to fully understand the long-term consequences of the Covid-19 pandemic. For the most part, we have had to talk in generalities: 'large scale' economic downturn, 'significant' pressure on the health, social care and education systems, and 'widespread' business closures. We probably won't truly know the full impact for years to come. What is clear, however, is that things will not be the same again for a long time indeed, and millions and millions of people will require some sort of long-term help.

On the plus side, there are clear signs of an enduring willingness to step up and help. Support for those on the front line of the pandemic response continues and there is still an army of citizens who are ready and willing to help and keep their communities going through the testing times. In the pre-pandemic days, 17% of the population went out of their way to 'put something back' every year. If you were to put a monetary value on the total number of hours volunteered, it would be £22 billion, according to the ONS. In the past year, it seems safe to say that this number will have increased many times over.

In the pre-pandemic days, the quest to make a difference meant everything from public demonstrations, whether it was teenagers giving up school to highlight climate change, to anti-capitalist marches, to protests against government policy. Meanwhile, nine million people donned bibs and ran to raise money for charity every year. On a less exhausting but no less noble level, hundreds of thousands of people gave up hours of their free time every month to volunteer, or just generally help out in their communities, doing everything from driving the elderly to hospital appointments, to helping out at the many historic properties, churches and gardens around the country. Once Covid-19 appeared, the focus of activities moved toward helping the NHS and local social groups. A veritable army of hundreds of thousands of citizens stepped up to register in organised groups, pledging to do what was required to help others during testing times. Others sought to plug the gaps in services and supplies by making PPE equipment for health workers, or making and delivering food and other goods to the elderly and vulnerable. Everywhere you look, there is no shortage of goodwill. Millions are doing something of their own to improve these inequalities.

If this describes you, and you're a regular and active volunteer or demonstrator, or even someone who is new to it, prompted into action at a time of great national need, that's great. There is now an opportunity to take your actions to the next level and make the time you give up work even more powerfully to help your chosen cause. What I am about to suggest will put you right at the centre of things, into a position where you are empowered to make real, positive changes towards the future. I am talking about becoming a board member so you can help influence meaningful social change from within. By signing up to be an independent director (ID), you will be getting right to the heart of what you care about the most. You will be able to oversee what an organisation does, see who it helps and how, and play a crucial role in delivering its services. IDs serve a vital role in any institution. They straddle that critical area between the top tier of management of that organisation and the users of its products and services. This is the opportunity to really make a difference in the causes you care the most about.

By taking a board role and becoming an ID, you can make the best use of your experience and skills to make meaningful changes in areas that personally resonate with you. You will be able to get into the centre of the action to sort out the problems from within. Most important, you will be able to use your passion for meaningful change and transform it into action.

Right now, there is no better time to consider becoming an independent director. The scale of the wider impact of Covid-19 on the economy and society as a whole is only now starting to emerge. While the pandemic was a public health crisis, the necessity for social distancing restrictions has dealt an unprecedented shock to all areas of our lives. Thousands of businesses have closed, with a corresponding impact on household incomes. Even where organisations have managed to survive, the financial impact on the millions of furloughed employees will be enduring. It adds up to a large amount of pressure on our welfare, health and social care systems, at a time when the government is scrabbling to catch up. At the same time, previously underfunded organisations in charity, the arts and community groups are at a breaking point. This is why the demand for impartial input is greater than ever before, and this demand is coming from a broader range of organisations, too. While at one time, independent directors were mainly associated with the corporate world, sitting on the boards of blue chip companies, all sorts of non-business and non-profit organisations now see value in the role. Many organisations are crying out for committed, passionate and experienced people to help. There are, for example, 170,000 charities in England and Wales and a similar number of sports clubs across the UK, all of which have governing bodies. The number of NHS Trusts runs into the hundreds and there are 130 universities in the UK. There are also positions in prisons, police authorities, government departments and housing associations all looking to strengthen their boards with IDs. In local communities, there are countless numbers of organisations, charities and advocacy groups in urgent need of support. If you are minded to become an ID, there are many, many directions to take.

The organisations in every sector were already under unbearable strain as a result of funding cuts following years of austerity before the pandemic. Meanwhile, the communities that public services seek to help are also buckling under the strain of vastly increased demand for services.

To understand the urgency, let's just look more closely at some of the challenges being faced by just some of the sectors mentioned here. I'll start with universities, a sector I am very familiar with thanks to my position as a member of the Council of the University of Exeter. While the University of Exeter is in robust financial health, it is the exception rather than the rule.

Universities had to plan for a 40% to 100% drop in international students in the year following the pandemic.[1] This is a crucial source of income for UK universities, totalling £13bn per annum, which are second only to the US in the number of international students it educates. International students make up half a million, or 20% of its entire student body.[2] There were many other reasons why so many universities were already spiralling into debt even before Covid-19. Since 1998, when tuition fees were first introduced, the financial burden of education has been shifting to the students who receive it, rather than on support from the government. When the fees were first introduced, they were capped at £1000 a year. Today, they are up to £9,250, although, subject to how the government implements the Augar Review, they may well see a highly significant reduction. While student numbers are still rising steadily, the freezing of student fees means that the income is not enough to sustain universities. The loss of government support is having a devastating impact on their bottom line.

To add to the pressure, since 2016, there has been a marked drop in the number of students enrolling from the European Union, thanks to the ongoing uncertainties around Brexit. Meanwhile, against all the advice from academics and advisors, the UK government included students in the target numbers for reduced immigration. As a result, the UK is now missing out on the revenue from thousands of international students. International students are amongst the most lucrative sources of income for universities. Both developments are costing universities and their local communities tens of millions in revenue every year.

In the past, when debt was cheaper, many universities launched aggressive expansion plans as a key part of their strategy to attract extra students. This could involve adding new buildings to UK campuses, or adding on a new satellite campus abroad. Millions have been borrowed from investors, with repayment projections relying on an ambitious growth in student numbers. However, with the cost of credit rising and those increased student numbers often failing to materialise, many universities are having to borrow more money to expand further, or simply to keep up with their current commitments.

Meanwhile, as with so many other sectors, the educational sector is grappling with an enormous pension deficit. The Universities Superannuation Scheme (USS), whose members include academics and higher education workers, was running at a £3.6 billion deficit.[3]

The effect of the economic consequences of Covid-19 means that this deficit is much higher. Proposed cuts to pensions have been met with loud protests and industrial action.

Under sustained pressure, many institutions have been tightening their belts and reigning in their spending. This means less investment in the quality of teaching and the calibre of staff, less investment in research and less investment in resources across the board. The result: a less satisfying, useful and fulfilling experience for students who quite rightly feel they are paying a great deal for their education and therefore deserve five-star service, whether it is in teaching, the quality of accommodation or additional sports and social facilities. The institutions that fail to find the right balance see student numbers plummet. This means that they reap lower fees and therefore have to cut their resources still further and see more disaffected students turn away. Sooner or later, the momentum of the downward plunge into debt becomes almost unstoppable.

The challenges are not going to go away. In fact, all the signs indicate that tuition fees are going to gain an ever-more prominent focus in politics in the coming years. The conservative government is, as previously noted, investigating whether or not to reduce student fees. What this means to the university sector is almost impossible to say, since no firm proposals have been floated, but there has been estimates that such a move could leave a £20 billion black hole in university finances. This hole is set to be even larger once the absence of international students is added to the mix. Where the money will come to fill that hole is yet to be seen. Given the enormous increase in the national debt to an estimated £300 billion, obtaining financial support from the government will be difficult. Suffice to say, every potential option seems dead-set to put an already beleaguered sector under more financial pressure. The sheer scale of the issues means that action is required now. Careful thought needs to be given to the make up of University Council members, and the people who join need to become deeply involved in understanding what is going on with these institutions.

> The people we need to come forward as IDs will hold the right values about the sector, whether it is a school or hospital or charity. They'll want the very best for that sector and they'll want to achieve it in a very transparent way.
>
> **Richard Atkins, Further Education Commissioner for England and Independent Member, Exeter University Council**

That the NHS is in as much if not more trouble than the higher education sector will come as no surprise to anyone. While the service coped brilliantly with the pandemic and garnered a much deserved and long overdue outpouring of public and political support, the problems and deficiencies of the nation's health service have been well-documented for years. Now though, the challenges are greater than ever before. Yet, according to new Henley Business School research, 20% of the people involved as either trustees or governors of the NHS say it is an impossible job to do. Think about that for one moment: *impossible*. Speak to anyone from the sporting, or charitable, or even education sectors, and they will say they face 'challenges' or that it is 'difficult' to find the right strategy. But 'impossible'?

Even before the pandemic, the mandate of the NHS was simply too large. Anyone can walk in and demand treatment, and there are simply not enough resources to fulfil this promise of universal healthcare. We have an ageing and growing population. Meanwhile, there are evolving healthcare needs with rises in cases of obesity and diabetes, together with increased antibiotic resistance. If admission rates continue to rise, we'll need an additional 6.2 million 'bed days' by 2022, which is the equivalent of 22 hospitals with 800 beds in each.[4] Although there are some brilliant medical advances which promise to save lives each year, they all cost money. In fact, progress in medical technology costs the NHS an extra £10 billion a year.

None of this will be news to anyone who has tried to access healthcare services in recent years. You may even be one of the nearly 500,000 a year who have faced delays of up to 18 weeks to start a planned treatment. Or perhaps even one of the tens of thousands who have had operations cancelled at the eleventh hour. In the first three months of 2018, a record 25,474 people were victims of this, with the Royal College of Surgeons blaming the increase on 'extreme pressures' on A&E departments and delayed discharges. Meanwhile, the four-hour A&E wait time target is to be scrapped, which is probably just as well since the NHS has not managed to hit the target since July 2015. The target will be replaced by, as yet unannounced, 'rapid care measures'. Even hospices are being forced to turn people away because they simply can't cope with demand.

> It's so easy to say: we're not putting enough money into the NHS. Well, it's actually a bottomless pit. There needs to be another way to effect change.
> **Dipti Amin, Independent Director, Cambridge Innovation Capital,**
> **University of Hertfordshire, Buckinghamshire Healthcare Trust**

Cuts in social care and a reduction in care homes is adding to the crisis each year. In the period between 2011/12 and 2016/17, the numbers of elderly people stuck in hospital beds while awaiting access to social care has rocketed by 209%.[5] Care homes were, of course, particularly hit by coronavirus, suffering more than a quarter of the known fatalities in the first months of the crisis, with claims that this sector was all but forgotten in the early efforts to stem the epidemic. In reality, this sector has been neglected for far too long beforehand and was already buckling under the pressure. In 2018, 101 care homes were declared insolvent after struggling with local authority budget cuts and increased staffing costs due to the rise in the national minimum wage from £7.50 to £7.83 in April 2018. Staffing issues are, of course, not an issue unique to social care. The number of vacancies in the NHS continues to hit record highs. In June 2018, the health service had 107,743 unfulfilled posts, up nearly 10,000 from just three months earlier. Within that was a shortage of almost 42,000 nurses, which is 12% of the entire workforce. Again, the problem has been exacerbated by Brexit fears and tougher immigration policies. But in yet another example of an uncontrolled downward spiral, the NHS is plugging the gaps in rotas by employing costly agency staff, costing £1.4 billion or more every quarter. At the same time, the turnover of staff they do have is higher than ever as medics leave the profession, unable to cope with the vastly increased work-load, difficult conditions and perceived lack of support.

With so much going on with staffing shortages and chronic underfunding, it would be easy to say: 'Well, what can be done?' Or, 'It's impossible', as the research found. Leave it up to the government to resolve the problem, right? Except, as we are all very aware, successive governments have done very little other than to repeat the mantra that the NHS is a lovely institution that should be protected at all costs. A Clap for Carers was added to these kind words during the coronavirus crisis. Yet, no one has really attempted to tackle the issues that are tearing it apart. It is for this reason that I truly believe that there is a clear role for the Board of Governors of individual NHS Trusts to step in and make basic changes. They have a key role to play in making the NHS function with the resources it has, challenging as that might sound. I know first-hand that supply chain experts have raised the issue of making the myriad of supply agreements held by each NHS Trust more efficient. One very well-informed source told me just recently that there is the very real possibility of revamping the outdated and cumbersome supply chain process. The critical shortage of personal protective clothing throughout the NHS and care homes that contributed to so many deaths of staff and patients is an example of this.

Why, also, is so little being invested in illness prevention? Just 0.5% of the annual budget is spent on prevention. Every car must have an annual MOT to ensure it is roadworthy and in the best condition, so why aren't NHS governors pushing hard for a 'human MOT' to be an important part of the strategy for patients? If we educate people about their diet and the importance of exercise, it can be a crucial first step to disease prevention. Perhaps then we could all be given the equivalent of an annual MOT, to check on our progress and give further advice and guidance. This is what will keep people out of hospital and which will reduce the pressure on the NHS. This has been personally brought home to me in recent months when the husband of a lady who works for me fell ill. He has been suffering from diabetes and, at the age of 70, is now going blind because of it. He may well not be in this situation today, along with the devastating effect it is having on both him and the family, if doctors had warned him about it and given guidance on how to prevent it. These ideas of active prevention and intervention are just two out of the many, but these are the sorts of measures which will break the momentum of out-of-control debt. Therefore, these are the ideas that boards of governors should be pushing hard to develop. Right now, I see very little sign of that. The reason has a great deal to do with the fact that the demands on the NHS are too great because the mandate is infinite.

So, if you would like the challenge of one of the most demanding independent director roles there are, then apply to become a trustee of an NHS Trust.

That's not the only option available though. Another prospect well worth considering is the charity sector, which saw a third of donations dry up overnight during the Covid-19 crisis. More than half of charities had to reduce existing levels of service, with others predicting they would have to do so in the future. A staggering 83% said that the only way they would survive in the medium-term would be through some sort of emergency grant funding.[6] Even before the pandemic, the charity sector was facing an unprecedented crisis in trust from donors. The Charities Aid Foundation (CAF) estimates the proportion of people giving money direct to charity dropped to 57% in 2018. That figure was 60% in the previous year and 61% in 2016.[7] Trust is at the heart of the downturn. The proportion of people who believe charities are trustworthy has fallen below 50%. You don't need to look very far to find out the reason why. The charity sector has been beset by a series of high-profile and galling scandals, many of which I will discuss in Chapter 4.

It appears that there is a lack of professionalism, skills and training among those at the top of many charities. If these issues are not addressed, we are going to see more and more scandals, and public trust will be further eroded. It's another downward spiral that needs to be stopped. We simply can't afford to let this happen. We owe that to the people these charities were set up to help. Once again, this is a sector crying out for new thinking at the top.

> In football, you need to have people on the board who are passionate about football and know all about it. You also need people who know business and how to run things effectively, efficiently and that make money. The game off the field is as important as the game on the field.
>
> **Jane Chafer, various ID positions including Plymouth Argyle,**
> **Sheffield International Venues, FX Plus**

Another sector to zero in on is sport. The pandemic upended the sporting calendar, with professional leagues everywhere suspending their activities to limit the spread of the virus among spectators. Even the Olympics of summer 2020 were postponed, depriving sports fans of one of the world's most-watched sporting broadcasts. But it wasn't just the big league athletes that were affected – every sports club, gym and athletic track across the nation has locked their gates. The reduction in revenue has impacted clubs large and small. There has already been a significant reduction in subscriptions as people cancel their memberships because of the crisis.

As with all the other sectors highlighted here, the sports sector was already grappling with its own set of issues before the coronavirus crisis. There has been a succession of stories about match fixing, sexual harassment and racism in football. In cricket, we've seen bribery and ball tampering. Stories have emerged of crooked admissions policies in elite athletic colleges, where families have been accused of cheating to get their children into places. The list of governance failures seems to just keep on growing.

Once you delve into the causes of the problems, the same issues arise again and again. The people who lead sporting organisations large and small are not skilled enough to prevent the abuses.

One of the major challenges that all of these organisations share in common (aside from the largest sporting clubs) is a lack of funding. There have been cuts everywhere, and they keep on coming. Since 2010, cumulative adult social care cuts have amounted to £7 billion.[8] In housing, the number of new homes built for social rent has fallen by almost four-fifths in a decade, with more than one million families stuck on waiting lists for council homes.[9] Funding for police in England and Wales fell by 19% between 2010 and 2019, after inflation is taken into account.[10] The list goes on.

With no signs of the cuts abating anytime soon – in fact, the opposite is more likely true as the government seeks to recoup some of the emergency pandemic spend – and organisations are already stretched to their limits and beyond, the focus is on getting more value out of the reduced budgets. To survive, let alone meet their purpose, services in every sector need to think hard about how they operate and to make sure their strategies are clearly defined. The goal is to optimise the impact of every pound. It's a huge challenge, but since change and innovation starts at the top, services across the board are crying out for effective leadership. Tough decisions need to be taken, but they need to be the right decisions.

While the problems many organisations face are writ large, there is a real dearth of recruits willing to put themselves forward to fill ID positions and help them work towards a solution. As we will see in Chapter 3, it is now widely recognised that a more diverse base of candidates is essential, yet not enough people are willing to volunteer their services. Often, the job is being left to people who have already retired and have time on their hands, when what is really needed to solve the huge problems facing many institutions is a wider range of age, backgrounds and skill sets. Quite simply, we need some fresh thinking.

One of the big problems a lot of organisations face is that, even though they have bought into the idea of diversity and are keen to bring in people with other perspectives, knowledge and a different way of thinking, they are not always able to find the right people. I've certainly had experiences where we've put out a brief to a recruitment agency specialising in roles in the not-for-profit sector, and they are not able to help. They do have a range of people on their books, but they keep having to go back to the same people. These people, quite rightly, are asking: 'Are they interested in me? Or are they interested in the fact I represent diversity?' It's almost having a negative effect.

Nobody wants to be seen as someone who is there to increase the diversity count. They want to know that they are valuable as individuals and sought out for specific skills. To solve this, we need more people to put themselves forward. However, organisations also need to think carefully about going down the blind alley of recruiting for diversity. They should be very clear about the characteristics and skills they are recruiting for, for that specific role, and then look at people from all backgrounds.

Helen Baker, current charity trustee roles include Shelter and The What Works Centre for Wellbeing

What are these organisations looking for? They want people like you. People who have a passionate interest in helping their community and in shaping the way the organisations that serve them are run. If you have the right skill set to add something to an organisation, as well as relevant experience and knowledge, that is what is important. And if you don't look like everyone else on the board, so much the better. No matter how diverse the board, it is the independence of thought that is most critical.

The majority of IDs roles are entirely voluntary, although some do pay basic expenses. They require anything from a few hours to several hours a month, but the difference it is possible to make is immeasurable. Without volunteers, many organisations would really struggle.

There are literally hundreds of opportunities in each local area, each of which will most likely welcome your input. It's important to realise that volunteering is not just a one-way street, though. While your selflessness should be applauded, the organisations you chose to help (and the people they are set up to help) are not the only beneficiaries. There are huge benefits to you, the volunteer. In fact, volunteering and the sense of purpose it brings with it, helps the people who step up in a vast number of ways. It's a great way to reduce stress, combat depression and provide mental stimulation. After many months in lockdown, that has to be a positive.

Let's just break that down a little bit further. There is barely a person in the modern world who wouldn't admit to regularly feeling stressed, angry and anxious, perhaps even more so today. There is evidence that being engaged in meaningful activities actively promotes feelings of wellbeing. Those that are absorbed in doing things they love experience positive emotions such as enthusiasm, cheerfulness, optimism, contentment and feel calm and relaxed.[11] Helping others, particularly those less fortunate, helps provide a new sense of perspective. Once you have a more positive outlook, it is easy to see things differently and revise your views on things that previously made you stressed.

Volunteering, corporate or otherwise, provides the perfect impetus to get out and connect with our local communities. Being part of an active social network gives us a feeling of belonging. Face-to-face activities, where you work closely with fellow board members, are a great way to reduce loneliness and isolation. You'll make life-long friends too.

The benefits gained from feeling that what you are doing is worthwhile cannot be underestimated either. Pride is a powerful motivator. Helping others naturally instils a sense of accomplishment. It connects you to your community too, because it gives you an identity.

Older adults, particularly those who have retired, can find new meaning in their life by looking after the interests of others. Those who still have a day job will discover that there are many career-enhancing opportunities here too.

Volunteering as an ID opens up the prospect of practicing a host of new and important skills which translate well back into the workplace: teamwork, communication, problem solving, project planning, task management and organisation. Even if you have some of these as existing skill sets, this is a great way to practice and improve upon them. If, say, you are a successful salesperson, you can work on improving your communication and marketing skills in a boardroom setting. There are benefits for the unemployed and carers too. Aside from being a chance to actively reconnect with the working world, the confidence boost gained from doing something worthwhile in a community cannot be underestimated.

Volunteering as an ID could well open up an entirely new career path. It's a chance to try out a new career without making the long-term commitment. Join an organisation that does the type of work you're interested in and 'road test' it as a suitable new direction. As you will see from the story that opens the next chapter, Helen Baker took her first ID roles as a way of keeping in touch with the work place as she brought up her young family. The initiative opened up an entirely new career path and one which she never left. As she says, her career advanced further because of her decision to volunteer.

What are your reasons for volunteering? After all, we all have plenty of things to do. The likely answer to why you and so many others do it lies in the title of this book: to make a difference. Indeed, a study of the motivations of regular volunteers revealed this to be an overriding priority. In one study, more than a third (36%) said they did it because they wanted to improve things and help people. The second reason (26%) was because the group, club or organisation really resonated with volunteers.[12] If you are predisposed to give up some of your time to help others, becoming an ID is the best way to make what you do *really* make a lasting difference. Best of all, it won't just make a difference to the organisations you help – it will be transformative for you, too.

Notes

1 https://www.theguardian.com/education/2020/apr/11/universities-brace-for-huge-losses-as-for eign-students-drop-out
2 https://www.marketplace.org/2020/05/12/covid-19-united-kingdom-universities-international-students/
3 https://www.ft.com/content/4aeff89c-100d-11e9-acdc-4d9976f1533b, 4 January 2019.
4 https://www.nuffieldtrust.org.uk/resource/nhs-hospitals-under-pressure-trends-in-acute-activ ity-up-to-2022, 6 October 2014.
5 https://www.ageuk.org.uk/latest-press/articles/2017/october/four-million-hospital-bed-days-lost-since-2011-due-to-problems-securing-social-care/, 18 October 2017.
6 https://www.institute-of-fundraising.org.uk/guidance/coronavirus/round-up-coronavirus-im pact-on-charities/

7 https://www.cafonline.org/docs/default-source/about-us-publications/caf-uk-giving-2018-report.pdf, March 2018.

8 https://www.theguardian.com/society/2019/may/24/austerity-social-care-charities

9 https://www.theguardian.com/society/2018/nov/22/construction-of-homes-for-social-rent-down-80-percent-on-a-decade-ago-england-families-waiting-lists

10 https://fullfact.org/crime/police-funding-england-and-wales/

11 https://www.mentalhealth.org.uk/publications/doing-good-does-you-good

12 https://www.ncvo.org.uk/images/documents/policy_and_research/volunteering/time_well_spent_ESV_report.pdf

Chapter 2
Good for me and good for you

Helen Baker's transition to roles on charity boards was partly borne out of necessity and partly out of a desire to give her career a boost. She began her working life as a social worker, managing community health teams in Westminster. When she took a career break to look after her children, she was keen not to stop working altogether. Deciding to take unpaid roles 'to keep her hand in', Helen's criteria for the roles she took was to find positions which would present a higher level of responsibility, and therefore risk, than she might otherwise have had, had she continued her previous career trajectory. Her motivation was to make an impact and to see how many people it is possible to reach by doing something positive.

'I took my professional skills and experience in the mental health sector and put them into another environment; the charity sector,' Helen explains. 'It gave me an experience of an entirely different side to things and the chance to continue to stretch myself professionally as well as to take on career development opportunities. I discovered that my skill set is more suitable to more strategic work, moving things along through other people. I enjoy inspiring, innovating and creating space for others to do really important things.'

'I took on my first chair role when I was about 30 years old and I have been chairing, or on the boards of charities in public sector bodies, ever since. I never actually went back to a full-time day job. I have done much more significant things in non-executive functions than I would have done in executive functions. Certainly, I've had infinitely more diverse and impactful responsibilities. Had I stayed on my original career path, I suppose I might have become a director of social services, but where would I have gone after that?'

Each of the organisations Helen has chaired has presented its own challenges. Here she describes her role at Dimensions, a charity providing personalised social care services for people with learning disabilities and autism, which she chaired until 2018.

'It is a large organisation with 7,000 staff all over the UK, a £190 million turnover and many subsidiaries and joint ventures too. There are many complexities to consider in running a charity like this that offer very high-intensity services to people with long-term disabilities, be it safeguarding risks, health and safety risks, staffing levels, public services contracts and so on.'

'It's a fast-paced environment. This means everyone on the board needs to be able to carry that level of complexity and work at a pace that keeps the organisation steady so it can deliver its purpose in a very challenging environment.'

Helen has developed her trustee role beyond that of chairing and sitting on charity boards. She has also set up charities, such as an organisation to help young

https://doi.org/10.1515/9783110706123-002

adults with dementia. In these cases, she will chair the boards initially and then step back to a smaller role on the board.

'The irony is, the more senior I have got in my career, the less I have been paid. My husband jokes that I've now achieved the pinnacle of my career: the status of working full-time for no income whatsoever. I can make an impact and have influence though. Much more so than in any of the executive roles I previously held.'

'When I left Dimensions, one of my colleagues said to me: 'Before you go, write a list of what you've done over the past five years. Write down the differences you have made.' I did and it was amazing. It was extraordinary to be a part of that.'

━

When weighing whether or not to take on an ID role, some people may find their decision falling at the first hurdle: time. As in: *I lead a very, very full life. I am not sure I can commit to x days a month indefinitely. It all seems too permanent.* For those in full-time employment, these reservations will no doubt be magnified many times over: *How can I ask my employer for regular time off to volunteer to serve on a board? They demand my full commitment at all times.* This may seem even more so today, when it is all hands to the pump to try and recoup some of the loses due to the extensive lockdown during 2020.

The good news is: If you are in full-time employment, there is no better time to step up and make the decision to serve as an ID elsewhere. It is probable that your employer will be 100% behind you. Why? Because employee engagement is *the* big thing in organisational development today. Engagement is the emotional commitment that connects people with the businesses they work for. It describes how they are inspired, motivated and energised, and why they stay loyal to their employer. As renowned business management psychologist Frederick Herzberg spelled out in his theory of motivation in the workplace: pay and working conditions can only ever *minimise* an employee's dissatisfaction with work. If you want to truly motivate a workforce, the team needs to be given a sense of responsibility, achievement and recognition. High on the list of priorities for the majority of the working population is to work for a company that cares about its impact on society. To feel fully committed to an organisation, individuals need to feel a sense of purpose and satisfaction. This is why Corporate Social Responsibility, or CSR, has become an important part of corporate culture for modern businesses. Companies all over the globe are looking closely at the impact they have on society and are putting ethical policies in place to support individuals, the local community and the environment. Among these initiatives, which range from fundraising to sustainability programmes, are corporate volunteering schemes for employees. Corporations recognise that volunteering makes people feel good about themselves and that it is hugely satisfying helping others, putting their skills to good use outside the workplace and contributing to the common good. Simply offering a few perks like a ping pong table or company away days is never going to be enough when it comes to fully engaging their workforce.

Perhaps not surprisingly, CSR has become a crucial front line in the war for the best talent. This goes for both recruitment and retention. According to one study, 64% of millennials won't accept a job at a company that doesn't have strong social responsibility practices.[1] More than one in ten would even take a pay cut to work for a company that has the right attitude toward charities.[2] Since this group will make up three-quarters of the workforce by 2025, it is a metric that can't be ignored. Today's talent only wants to work with organisations that are willing to make a positive impact on the world and that respond to the current pressures upon it following the pandemic.

When it comes to keeping people engaged – and therefore ensuring they stick around for the long haul – there needs to be evidence that the employer is ready to give back. Even before the coronavirus crisis, over half (57%) of UK employees said they wanted their employers to do more for CSR and 63% said paid time off during working hours for charitable initiatives would significantly improve their engagement. It's not a 'like to have', either – 51% believe their company has a duty to commit to charitable acts and CSR.[3]

The pressure to reach out into communities does not just come from within. Social responsibility is a priority in the wider world. Consumers have a growing expectation that the companies they buy from will seek to make a positive impact on their local communities, over and above purely commercial considerations. Three-quarters of the public now believe it is either very important or absolutely essential for companies to act in a responsible way.[4] We are all prepared to put our money where our mouths are too: 88% of consumers are more likely to buy from a business that visibly acts to improve society.[5] My suspicion is, with the increased social awareness there is now, these figures will only go up.

> It's all a matter of negotiation when it comes to the main job. Whilst it is increasingly becoming the norm for employers to allow up to 20 days away from the office for ID roles, this is still very much determined on a case-by-case basis. It helps to present it as part of a personal development plan to support the development of specific insights or skills. People sometimes forget that having support for these roles, does need to benefit their employer in some way shape or form, too.
>
> **Michelle Leavesley, ID Warwickshire CCC, Sport & Play Construction Association, British Wheelchair Basketball**

If none of these arguments are enough to sway an employer of the advantages of engaging their team through initiatives allowing them to volunteer as IDs, there two more very powerful arguments. The first is to do with the factor that drives any commercial organisation: profit. CSR initiatives have been revealed to have a markedly positive impact on the bottom line. Research shows that companies with a fully engaged workforce outperform their peers by 147% in earnings per share.[6] (Extrapolate that further for a moment: if the productivity of the UK workforce went up by just 1%, the economy would save approximately £17 billion).[7] Engaged employees are also more likely to perform better, take 3.5 fewer sick days a year, and stick around longer than their disengaged colleagues. Since being allowed to volunteer is central to engagement, this means there are not many forward-thinking employers that would dismiss out-of-hand a request to volunteer.

The second reason is to do with the rules and obligations impacting large- and medium-sized organisations. For a while it looked like corporate volunteering would be enshrined in law, after prime minister David Cameron made it a manifesto pledge in 2015 as part of his 'big society' vision. His goal was to introduce three days of annual paid volunteering leave for all those employed in companies with over 250 people. Sadly, this was not to be enacted. However, while it is not a legal requirement for companies to undertake many of their CSR activities, there are other rules in place that mean companies are expected to report on a range of social, environmental and ethical issues. This has opened the door to a greater support for voluntary activities. Under the Companies Act 2006, one of the duties of all directors is to promote the success of their company for the benefit of its team. This means CSR issues should feature in the boardroom on a regular basis. Among the many areas of discussion, which include frequent scrutiny that the needs of employees are being met, is also to explore the impact of the company's operations on the community and the environment.

The Companies, Partnerships and Groups (Accounts and Non-Financial Reporting) Regulations 2016 says that quoted companies and financial institutions in particular must include information in their strategic reports describing their approach to environmental matters, employees and social, community and human rights issues. This report must also include information about any policies of the business in this respect and also the success and effectiveness of its policies.

The clear evidence of the merits of employee engagement and the rules governing greater CSR awareness have all greatly strengthened the cause of CSR. Employees are in a stronger position than ever when it comes to asking their workplace for support in voluntary activities. The response will most likely be positive too. Indeed, many businesses already have extensive programmes in place. Indeed, employer-supported volunteering (ESV), where employees of an organisation are given paid time off to volunteer during working hours is becoming the norm, particularly in large companies. (The highest number of ESV schemes are found in businesses employing over 1,000 people.) The practice is also gaining traction elsewhere in forward-thinking small- and medium-sized enterprises. ESV initiatives broadly fall into two categories. The first is where employees can actively choose the charity or community group they'd like to support. Alternatively, the employer can make a recommendation of their own, perhaps because of a prior link with the organisation in question. Right now, the most frequent form of ESVs tends to be short-term support for charity events, such as pulling together a team to run a local marathon in the name of a charity, or spending an away day helping to tidy and plant-out a children's area in a playground. Around 30% of ESV-volunteers participate in such one-off events.[8] There is, however, take up on long-term volunteering opportunities, albeit at a lesser scale. This is where we find initiatives to encourage team members to volunteer as charity trustees or school governors, with 16% of ESV volunteers becoming trustees or members of committees.[9]

If employers are willing to run ESV programmes, the big question is: How much time will they give their employees to volunteer? Plus, how will it impact the employee's pay? The evidence seems to show that, over and above the odd charity day, the majority of companies are still reluctant to offer any paid time off. More than three-fifths of UK employees (63%) are not getting paid if they take time off to volunteer. Some industries are less receptive to the idea than others too. Thus, those working in healthcare, architecture, engineering and building might struggle to convince employers of the merits of paid time off (75% don't get paid time to volunteer). However, if you are in professional services, the arts and culture industries, around a quarter (24%) get at least a one day off per year. Geography plays a part too. Among organisations in London, 41% of staff report being allowed time off to volunteer. Compare this to Scotland, where 75% say they are unable to take any time off for CSR activities.[10] I should add that these are pre-pandemic figures and we don't yet know for sure how organisations will react to whatever the new normal turns out to be. They may be much more inclined to support voluntary endeavours, or, with employee numbers down, much less able to accommodate requests. Time will tell.

Among the companies that offer paid volunteering days, the majority offer just one day off per year. There are organisations that offer more days off and, quite rightly, draw attention to it in their recruitment literature. Experian, the credit bureau, offers three paid days a year, as does consulting firm Accenture, while accounting and payment systems company Sage offers five. Insurance giant Allianz allows employees ten hours paid leave per year for a volunteering activity of their choice.

The number of days an individual employer is willing to allow individuals to take off needn't be a deal-breaker when it comes to pursuing ID roles on governing bodies or boards. Many organisations looking for volunteers are fully aware of the potential barriers and will do their best to hold at least some meetings in the evenings or late in the day. In other cases, board volunteers may need to be innovative. One idea might be to secure the support of employers by offering a holiday matching deal. In other words, if the volunteer takes one day out of their holiday entitlement to volunteer, the employer could match the gesture by offering an extra day in lieu. The important thing is to start the discussion. As shown here, businesses are receptive to the idea of people on their teams corporate volunteering, since the merits of ESV are hard to ignore. It offers benefits all round.

No one should be afraid to step up and request the support of their employers in their goal to service their communities, particularly at a time of very clear need. Sadly though, at this moment, there is clear evidence that this is not being talked about enough. While ESV participation is growing and around 10% of volunteers now do so via these programmes, not enough people are taking advantage of the opportunity. Some reports show that even where businesses are giving employees the green light to volunteer, many people are ignoring the offer. Some reports show that where employees have a scheme available, just a quarter to a third participate at least once a year.[11]

We need to start that conversation and make sure that more people are not just allowed to volunteer, but are actively encouraged to do so. Plus, on the flip side to this, individuals should not be reluctant to press employers for their support. There are no doubts that it is to everyone's advantage. The simple message is: If businesses focus on their employees' wellbeing and happiness, they will do better and society will be better off too. Happiness is derived from a sense of ownership and control and feeling positive about the environment in which you work.

Notes

1 https://www.telegraph.co.uk/business/ready-and-enabled/why-corporate-social-responsibility-is-important/

2 https://www.hrmagazine.co.uk/article-details/csr-could-be-the-key-to-boosting-engagement-and-productivity-research-suggests

3 https://www.hrreview.co.uk/hr-news/strategy-news/poor-employee-engagement-costing-uk-businesses-upwards-of-17bn/20345

4 http://www.smf.co.uk/publications/more-than-cv-points-the-benefits-of-employee-volunteering-for-business-and-individuals/

5 https://volunteeringmatters.org.uk/app/uploads/2015/04/CSV-Employee-Volunteering-Who-is-Benefitting-Now.pdf

6 https://www.gallup.com/workplace/229424/employee-engagement.aspx?utm_source=gbj&utm_medium=copy&utm_campaign=20160922-gbj

7 https://www.hrmagazine.co.uk/article-details/csr-could-be-the-key-to-boosting-engagement-and-productivity-research-suggests

8 https://www.ncvo.org.uk/images/documents/policy_and_research/volunteering/time_well_spent_ESV_report.pdf

9 https://www.ncvo.org.uk/images/documents/policy_and_research/volunteering/time_well_spent_ESV_report.pdf

10 https://www.employeebenefits.co.uk/three-fifths-employees-volunteer/

11 https://www.ncvo.org.uk/images/documents/policy_and_research/volunteering/time_well_spent_ESV_report.pdf

Chapter 3
Making a difference starts with a new perspective

Everybody is more accountable today. There is more information published about the performance of schools, hospitals are judged by how quickly people are seen and businesses are increasingly competitive. It means there is a constant pressure to improve. In this age of accountability, organisations in every sector need to look to bring together the absolute best selection of skills and experience into the boardroom. They need a good mix of backgrounds too.

**Richard Atkins, Further Education Commissioner for England
and Independent Member, Exeter University Council**

It's an incontrovertible fact that great organisations (whatever the size) have great management committees behind them. But what are 'great management committees'? What has been shown time and time again to work best is a good mix of people with a range of skills, and a track record in a similar or complementary discipline. It helps if individuals on those committees have some knowledge of general management and risk too. Most of all though, to be truly effective, a board needs to be diverse. When something goes wrong in an organisation (and we'll see a dizzying array of past failures in the next chapter) one of the major contributing factors in every instance (if not *the* major contributing factor) is that the boards were full of people with a similar background and viewpoint. With everyone thinking the same, there is less chance of anyone challenging the status quo. Abuses go unchecked, discrepancies are ignored and bad decisions are nodded through.

Diversity of age, experience, gender, ethnicity, disability, approach and personality are all key to good governance and decision-making. It guarantees new thinking, insights and perspectives about customers, markets and business practices.

My own first experience of the benefits of diversity came in 1998, when Dennis Gillings invited me to join the board of Quintiles, an international leader in clinical development and commercial outsourcing services to the biopharmaceuticals industry. Dennis and I had both been students at the University of Exeter. However, while the fact that I believe that personal relationships really do matter in business did encourage me to take up the offer, that was not my only motivation. I was also encouraged by his passionate support of diversity on boards. My background was in logistics, which was a different industry entirely, and Dennis also appointed a woman from a biotechnology business who had extensive experience in Corporate Social Responsibility. The various different perspectives meant we had a high-quality board which provided a different level of scrutiny and advice. I was completely sold on the benefits of diversity.

In any organisation, there is a big element of needing to know the subject and the industry it operates in. But then, as with anything in life, it is useful to get an external opinion. Whether or not that opinion changes the direction of travel, or simply provides another viewpoint, it makes

https://doi.org/10.1515/9783110706123-003

everyone consider things more deeply. It stops mistakes being made. That is why diversity is so important.

Liz Johnson, Board Member, Disability Sport Wales

For any organisation focussed on the bottom-line (and what organisation isn't, even in the not-for-profit sector? Businesses do need to be viable, after all), there are sound financial reasons for backing diversity. McKinsey & Company's *Delivering Through Diversity* report[1] has established a strong correlation between boardroom diversity and financial performance. While this particular study focuses on corporates, there are some interesting lessons that could be interpreted in the health/charity/sports/education sectors. According to the report, organisations in the top quartile for gender diversity of their executive teams were 21% more likely to experience above-average profitability than those in the fourth quartile. When it comes to ethnic/cultural diversity, that figure rises to 33%. By the same token, organisations which were the least diverse in terms of both gender and ethnic diversity, were 29% more likely to *underperform* on profitability than their more enlightened counterparts in the other quartiles.

It's not just about money, though. Well, at least not in a direct way. Diversity is key in the war for talent. A diverse and inclusive boardroom speaks volumes when it comes to the ability to attract, develop and retain talent. Every organisation around the world is having to compete in the face of a range of new challenges. We operate in a highly digital environment, on a global scale, in the face of ever-tighter budgets. This is before we get to the challenge of rebuilding our businesses and communities following the coronavirus crisis. Every organisation, large and small, needs access to the largest pool of talent possible if they are to compete effectively in this changing world. Potential recruits will look at institutions to see if there are other people like them there. Will they be welcome? Will they fit in? If the make-up of the board signals a firm 'no', they'll look to take their services elsewhere. It stands to reason that any organisation will be at a competitive disadvantage if they cannot attract the best possible talent.

To further broaden out this idea, let's consider the reputational issues that are at stake. Whenever a new scandal occurs at any organisation, whether in the corporate world or not-for-profit sector, I find myself looking up the Annual Report of the organisation involved, or turning to the online 'about us' section. When I find the pictures of the boardroom line up, I invariably find myself utterly unsurprised when I see the usual row upon row of middle-aged or older, white male faces staring out at me from the photos. I know I am not alone in my cynicism about this issue. Any organisation that wants to improve its standing among *all* of its stakeholders, whether it is customers, employees, communities or society as a whole, needs to address this issue.

There is also clear evidence that a diverse board improves the quality of decision-making by introducing a new perspective which can lead to improved, more accurate group thinking. There was an interesting study by the *Journal of Personality and Social Psychology*[2] where scientists assigned people to six-person mock jury panels. The panels were made up of a range of different backgrounds, with some being all white, others with four white and two black volunteers and so on. The juries were then all showed a video of a trial concerning a black defendant and white victims. The subsequent deliberations were very revealing. The more diverse panels were more focussed on the facts when discussing vital evidence and made fewer factual errors than the homogenous panels. If any errors did occur, they were more likely to be corrected in the discussion.

To correlate how this might work in a board setting, there is another useful study that analysed approximately 600 corporate decisions made by 200 different business teams over a range of companies in the space of two years.[3] The research found that inclusive teams made better decisions 87% of the time. These teams also made their decisions twice as quickly, and with half the number of meetings required. The decisions made delivered 60% better results. The study also drilled into the impact derived from the make-up of the teams. It found that, compared to individual decision-makers, all-male teams made better decisions 58% of the time. Gender diverse teams beat that by doing so 73% of the time. To make better decisions 87% of the time, you'd need a team composed from both sexes, a range of ages and from different geographical locations.

> The traditional board has often been predominantly white and male. They have also been risk-averse. If something's thought to be a jolly good idea, they all go down the same path, and they'll all agree. This is in great part down to the fact it is actually quite difficult for somebody who is the same as everybody else to disagree with their colleagues.
>
> In the university and charity sector, boards can operate in their own bubbles. In universities, for example, the council can be dominated by university leadership and academics. They know all about teaching and research, but they won't know anything about risk and financial management and how to keep their heads above water in challenging times.
>
> Once you start getting diversity things change. Someone with a different perspective might say, *Have you thought about the effect this action might have upon this particular group? Don't you think we should review this?* It stops things plodding along as they have always done.
>
> It can't just be a box-ticking exercise. Adding a single token woman or ethnic minority to the board is completely ineffective. This gives everyone else the space to group together, roll their eyes and dismiss the lone voice as 'going off on one'. You need two or three different new faces to start making a tangible difference.
>
> **Sarah Turvill, Chair of Council, University of Exeter**

Better, more considered, decision-making means less reckless risk-taking. Even though it happened more than ten years ago, the 2008 global credit crunch and the chaos that ensued is still fresh in everyone's minds. In all the enquiries that followed, there was a clear path leading to an appalling, unchecked excess of reckless risk-taking by testosterone-fuelled bankers who were mainly led by all-white male boards. A diverse team at the top ensures multiple views are taken on the outcome of any proposed action, which naturally leads everyone involved to examine and discuss the potential risks. Firms with more diverse boards are more likely to be able to properly evaluate risks. In the case of a publicly quoted company, this in turn translates into a greater likelihood of dividends for stockholders and higher dividends per share at that.

Harvard Business Review, which studied board diversity in its report *Why Diverse Teams are Smarter*,[4] concluded that diverse teams are more prone to re-examining facts while also remaining objective. It speculated that breaking up homogeneity forces people to become more aware of their unconscious biases, which might tie them into strenuously supporting one way of thinking, even when the evidence points in entirely another direction.

It's not always easy for an organisation to change intrenched habits and hire individuals who don't look, talk or think like everyone else on the board. This is particularly so if things have been the same as far back as anyone can remember. Remember though: the cost of conformity is that it discourages innovative thinking. It's too easy to fall back into the position of: why change, when no one can think of anything different to do? Enriching a board with a mix of different genders, races, ages, skills and experience and nationalities will boost its creative potential to develop new ideas. Each member will bring new perspectives and approaches when it comes to solving complex, or unexpected, non-routine problems. Many of those Covid-19 volunteers who may never have considered stepping up before will have learned valuable skills from the experience and this is an opportunity to put them to further good use.

Despite the clear sign posts pointing to the benefits of diversity on boards, there is a long way to go. Let's take the gender divide as a starting point. In recent years, there have been greater moves to increase women's representation on FTSE 100 and FTSE 250 boards. According to the latest figures available, progress is being made, but far, far too slowly. Since October 2017,[5] the percentage of women on FTSE boards is up from 27.7% to 29%. Progress on FTSE 250 boards is marginal though – 23.7%, up from 22.8%. If the current pace continues, we were expected to meet a target of 33% by 2020. The figures here do contain good news for female ID positions, which are at an all time high of 35.4% in FTSE 100 businesses. Unfortunately, executive positions appear to have flatlined at 9.7%, so there is still a way to go there. Those hoping for more diverse boards can also be encouraged by the number of female IDs now chairing committees. Eighty-five women chair 95 committees, with the majority (42) chairing remuneration and a further 23 chairing audit/risk committees. However, before breaking out the bunting to celebrate, I should add that 253 male IDs chair 293 committees.

The diversity picture on NHS boards is more positive on face value when it comes to gender profile. NHS Foundation Trusts average around 14 members, with the balance swinging to slightly more executive directors than non-executives.[6] Women comprise just under 43% of NHS provider board members, although the

NHS has signed up to achieve the goal of 50:50 by 2020. It should be noted that the split is much more even at executive level (52% v 48%), whereas women make up a much smaller proportion of IDs (62% v 38%). It is also perhaps worth weighing all of these figures against the fact that 77% of the health service workforce are women.

Charities suffer from a similar disparity as that in the health sector. Whilst women make up 65% of charity employees, they number 43% of the total trustees in the top 500 charities.[7] However, as ever, drill down further into the figures and they make even more depressing reading. There are thirty all-male charity boards, versus just one all-female board.

Like all the sectors highlighted here, universities are just as ambitious with their gender diversity targets. English universities were aiming for a 40% female representation on their boards by 2020 and Scottish universities were aiming to go higher at 50% by the same target date. It remains to be seen how the pandemic affected these projections. Overall, there's some way to go, whatever happens. Women still make up just 36% of university boards and chair just 19% across the UK.[8]

Women in Sport has had some success with its Beyond 30% campaign, which aims to ensure that every publicly funded National Governing Body of sport (NGB) has a minimum of 30% of one gender represented on its board. While they have hit the average figure of 30%, there are still worrying figures underlying that average.[9] Nine of the 68 NGBs surveyed by Women in Sport, which fall under the Sport England umbrella, have no women at all in senior leadership roles, excluding CEO, and one has no women in any sort of leadership position at all. There has been an overall fall in women in senior leadership roles since 2014 (42% down to 36%) and evidence to show the pipeline of women in these roles has stalled.

And what of ethnicity? The figure to bear in mind here is the percentage of people from Black, Asian and Minority Ethnic (BAME) backgrounds in the UK is 14%. Just 84 of the 1,048 director positions in the UK's largest companies are held by a business leader from an ethnic minority, and this figure is down one point from the previous year. There are just five ethnic minority CEOs and the majority (54%) of FTSE 100 boardrooms still show no evidence of any ethnic diversity at all.

In the charity sector, in which over half of the top 500 charities have a combined income of £35.5 billion, the situation seems even more bleak. Something that I find very significant is research which shows that the largest charities in England and Wales have less diverse boards than FTSE 100 firms, which themselves are often accused of being overwhelmingly 'pale, male and stale'. A 2018 analysis by Inclusive Boards[10] found just 6.3% of board members were from black, Asian, or minority ethnic backgrounds, compared with 8.2% among the FTSE 100 companies. A staggering 62% of the top 500 charities are comprised of all-white boards. The least likely group to be represented were women of colour. For a sector which brands itself on fairness, compassion and inclusion, championing the rights of some of the most marginalised in society, this is simply not good enough.

The trend in charities is going in the wrong direction, too. In a recent survey, figures show that the number of all BAME boards has halved to four, while there has been a 5% increase in all-white boards.[11] In sport, it is a similar story: the average percentage of people on boards from a BAME background is 4%.[12] The pattern is repeated in the NHS, with BAME being underrepresented in board membership, taking just 7.7% of roles, but 45% of NHS boards have no BAME members at all. Again, it is worth noting that staff from BAME backgrounds account for 17.7% of NHS roles.

Disability is another area of diversity that can't be ignored. There are more than 12 million people in the UK with a disability. According to the ONS, around 8% of the population consider themselves to be 'limited a lot' by disability, while a further 9% say they are 'limited a little'. Figures on the representation of disabled people on corporate boards are hard to come by, which in itself speaks volumes. We mostly need to rely on anecdotal evidence – can you name a disabled CEO? In sport, it has been reported that the percentage of disabled people on NGB boards is 3%, while the percentage of people who identify as disabled on NHS boards is 5.3%, although there is a split which is slightly higher in non-executive roles. The charity sector appears to be doing a little better, with disabled board-level representation at 10%, according to Henley Research.

Last and by no means least, one further crucial area to consider in the context of diversity is age. For some reason, while it is fairly well known that the vast majority of board members are of a certain age, age diversity does not seem to attract the same attention as other forms of diversity. Again, data is scarce, but it is believed that the percentage number of IDs under 50 is in single figures. PwC's research into the US market shows that just 6% of directors are in this age bracket in the S&P500.[13] This seems a ludicrous dichotomy since we know Generation Z (those born between 1996 and 2010) are keen to volunteer and, as we've already seen, employers are opening up opportunities to do so via ESVs.

Does it matter? Well, yes, it does. Yet again, the younger generation, though not a homogenous group, is a cohort that can bring fresh skills and perspectives. Take technology skills as a case in point. This generation has grown up in the midst of the greatest shift in the way things are done since the Industrial Revolution. They understand digital transformation, data and analytics and know its value. It stands to reason that they are in a good place to assist boards to adopt new opportunities and challenges. Don't forget, either, that many of their customers and stakeholders will be from this generation. It makes sense to have people on board who are closer to their experiences and speak their language.

In the past, the obvious retort has been that people simply didn't have time. Women and men from this generation have been busy building their careers and raising families. That left little time over to serve on boards and be an effective presence. We now live in a very different world. Many people who were furloughed during the pandemic didn't have jobs to go back to. With widespread company closures, unemployment has soared. While troubling on a personal and professional basis, this could represent a big opportunity for people to take the first steps back into the workplace and to learn valuable new skills at the same time. Even for those who are still working, ID roles can still be a crucial part of career development. Anyone who feels strongly about making a difference in a particular field could and should make time – certainly enough time for a single appointment. Plus, many employers are increasingly seeing the developmental value in allowing members of their team to volunteer for board-level roles elsewhere.

One of the most fantastic things we've done with Leap (an organisation that supports disadvantaged young people and helps them to make changes in their lives) was to pioneer putting young people on the board. By young, I mean from the age of 18. These were young people who had been through Leap's programme and fully understood what it was trying to achieve. We put a lot of thought and effort into how we do this. For example, we made sure there were two or three young people on the board, so they didn't feel like they were on their own. When I was chair, either the CEO or I would spend a lot of time with them ahead of each board meeting, making sure they looked at the board papers and discussed any aspects they wanted to make points on. During the meetings, I was careful to bring them in naturally, to invite their contribution so they did not feel intimidated.

We repeated the experience at the EY Foundation. In the last round of recruitment for the Youth Advisory Board, we received more than 200 applications. The reason for this is because their predecessors had a good experience of being on the board. Young people know that they are not just there as a token – they are actually going to personally develop because of it. We are very clear with them that this is a very serious thing that they are signing up for. We really want them to understand what is going on.

Patrick Dunne, ID roles include Boardelta, EY Foundation, ESSA and Leap

While the perceived advantage to be derived from more diverse boards is gaining traction, and there are many targets in place, there is still a long way to go. Indeed, while there have been pockets of progression toward more diversity, it is sad to see that some of momentum has understandably stalled a little in the light of the pandemic. The onus now is on the boards themselves to actively seek out and recruit a wider range of representation, but this doesn't mean that as many people as possible shouldn't step up to the plate and put themselves forward. Ultimately, the more momentum we can get, the better.

The fact is, boards which are genuinely interested in increasing diversity will need to look beyond the usual pool of candidates. To find these valuable new perspectives, it's very likely that they'll need to recruit people who might have had no previous board experience. This might entail scrutiny of potential candidates who might be slightly lower in the hierarchy, perhaps as general managers, division heads, or who have worked at a senior level in universities, charities and sporting bodies. There may be a focus on retirees who have previously led large government agencies, or stepped down from the military or emergency services. There will also be a need for a great deal of lateral thinking. While interviewing for this book, I spoke to a number of recruiters who were all actively looking to recruit IDs with very specific skills, such as in digital, turnaround or money raising. There was less of a focus on a candidate's previous experience in senior roles and more on their specific skills and knowledge. This, I believe, can only be a good thing, since the broader brief will naturally encourage greater diversity.

Notes

1 https://www.mckinsey.com/~/media/mckinsey/business%20functions/organization/our%20insights/delivering%20through%20diversity/delivering-through-diversity_full-report.ashx, January 2018.

2 Sommers, Samuel R., On Racial Diversity and Group Decision-Making: Identifying Multiple Effects of Racial Composition on Jury Deliberations. *Journal of Personality and Social Psychology*, Vol. 90, pp. 597–612, 2006. Available at SSRN: https://ssrn.com/abstract=940788

3 https://www.cloverpop.com/hacking-diversity-with-inclusive-decision-making-white-paper?utm_campaign=Forbes&utm_source=Forbes&utm_medium=Forbes%20Hacking%20Diversity%20White%20Paper, September 2017.

4 https://hbr.org/2016/11/why-diverse-teams-are-smarter, November 2016.

5 http://business-school.exeter.ac.uk/media/universityofexeter/businessschool/documents/research/Female_FTSE_Report_2018.pdf

6 https://improvement.nhs.uk/documents/2620/NHSI_board_membership_2017_survey_findings_Oct2018a_ig.pdf

7 http://www.inclusiveboards.co.uk/charity-governance-2018/

8 https://www.theguardian.com/higher-education-network/2018/mar/28/universities-government-targets-female-representation-boards

9 https://www.womeninsport.org/wp-content/uploads/2017/10/Women-in-Sport-Beyond-3025-1-1.pdf?x99836, February 2017.

10 http://www.inclusiveboards.co.uk/charity-governance-2018/, 19 April 2018.

11 http://www.inclusiveboards.co.uk/charity-governance-2018/

12 http://www.sportbusinesscentre.com/wp-content/uploads/2018/03/FINAL-REPORT-the-state-of-sports-governance.pdf, March 2018.

13 https://www.pwc.com/us/en/services/governance-insights-center/library/younger-directors-bring-boardroom-age-diversity.html, January 2019.

Chapter 4
Stop the rot. Scandals start at the top. Always.

Big organisations are successful because they get very good at doing the same thing over and over again. That doesn't last forever. Inviting an ID in, who hasn't been doing that thing over and over again, is an opportunity to see a different perspective on the same old problems.

Richard Sargeant, Chief Commercial Officer, Faculty; ID, Exeter University; Government Centre for Data Ethics and Innovation

What is behind this urgent plea for more people to get involved and make a difference? Clearly, we are in the midst of what will be a lengthy recovery phase from the Covid-19 crisis, and many organisations are operating in entirely new and unknown territories. It is my belief that the role of IDs will become more important than ever as we all work out the best way forward. IDs have an essential role to play in challenging the wider decisions of boards and ensuring that what they do is in the best interests of all the communities they serve. Their purpose has developed far beyond that of a 'box-ticking' exercise as part of good governance. The skills they bring are needed to transform the direction of the organisations whose boards they advise on.

The reason this is so important today is because we don't want any of these volunteers' efforts going to waste. Even before Covid-19, no one could escape the depressingly regular headlines documenting the appalling personal cost of our badly under-managed health system. Nor could we ignore the relentless news of large-scale job losses, thanks to a succession of corporate scandals where the losers always seemed to be the people who worked for large firms, rather than the executives who were at the helm. Even the charities that so many fundraisers tried to help might also provoke a certain feeling of uneasiness, thanks to damaging governance stories about leading charities such as Kids Company and Oxfam. We can't even rely on the next generation being any better off, thanks to elements of the university sector being in apparent tatters and offering seemingly less value for money to fee-paying students.

In this chapter, I would like to highlight the potential penalties of doing nothing, or leaving things to someone else to sort out. Letting it be someone else's problem makes for ineffective management committees. To show just how pervasive ineffectiveness can be, I will share the wide range of ways where IDs could have, yet failed to make, an impact, whether it was down to lack of passion, skills or something more sinister. I have compiled my top ten list of some of the worst outcomes of a lack of leadership and governance. I've illustrated them with a rogue's gallery of scandals from recent years, all of which have come from the sectors I have been talking about here. In each case, the downfall has been facilitated by a crippling lack of oversight from management committees.

https://doi.org/10.1515/9783110706123-004

Executive pay abuses

Unease abounds at the inflated salaries awarded to top executives of organisations. They occur with depressing frequency in every sector. To understand how pervasive it can be, let's look at the impact in education. According to figures from the higher education regulator in England, the Office for Students (OfS), university debt has trebled over the past decade to £12 billion and by some estimates, 20% of UK universities are currently experiencing financial difficulties. In the summer of 2018, the OfS was forced to bail out one unnamed university to the tune of £900,000 when it became at serious risk of running out of money. International credit rating agency Moody's has told its clients that there is a high probability that this won't be a one-off.[1] Indeed, there have been reports that up to three universities are on the brink of bankruptcy.[2] Once again, these figures were from a pre-pandemic environment. The current situation is far bleaker.

Yet, with all this going on, there's long been ample evidence of just how out of touch some university councils have become. There have been some, quite frankly, bonkers pay awards to some university leadership. In 2017, Dame Glynis Breakwell's status as the UK's highest paid university leader caused an outcry and the vice-chancellor of Bath University eventually agreed to step down after extensive protests. It was not just the fact that she was the UK's highest-paid head that had observers crying foul, nor the apparent contrast with the relatively modest size of the university she presided over. What concerned many people was the fact the controversial £468,000 pay package was approved by Bath's University Council Remuneration Committee, which she herself sat on. It can't be escaped that this somewhat chummy relationship would have had an impact on discussions.

> When I see colleges that are not doing well, governance is usually at the root of the problem. Often, there are governors who have been there far too long. They haven't kept to two or three terms of office over six to ten years. Being on the governing body for far longer, they have a relationship with the chief executive that's far too cosy. They don't challenge much or keep up to date with the national standards, or with what is going on elsewhere in other institutions. They become too inward-looking, passive participants that go along with whatever the chief executive recommends.
>
> There may be one or two, perhaps newer governors who realise things are not quite right, but it is difficult to bring about change quickly in an environment like that.
>
> **Richard Atkins, Further Education Commissioner for England and Independent Member, Exeter University Council**

Accounting irregularities

The ironic part of accounting *irregularities* is that they appear to be occurring rather too *regularly*. Often, concerns are raised and then completely ignored until it is too late. Issues with funding, performance and management were certainly enough to close the Kids Company charity in August 2015. The organisation, founded in 1996 in south London, had initially been set up to provide emotional, practical and educational support to deprived and vulnerable inner-city children and had many high-profile supporters, including former prime minister David Cameron. Concerns over problems at the charity were raised as far back as 2002, however, the National Audit Office reported that the charity had received at least £46 million of public money despite these concerns, all apparently overseen by a committee of high-profile volunteer trustees. When it abruptly closed, Kids Company had 11 centres in London and Bristol and was working with more than 40 schools. Emergency plans had to be implemented to support the vulnerable children who were affected. In the post-mortem that inevitably followed, various parties were blamed, including the charity's trustees, the chair Alan Yentob and its founder Camila Batmanghelidjh, but no one was willing to admit responsibility for the failing.

Tax evasion

There has been much in the press about the tax policies of Facebook, Apple and Google which have come under scrutiny even from their own shareholders, thanks to widespread concerns that tax avoidance strategies are reputation damaging, as well as being detrimental to the communities they operate in. The practice is not just confined to large corporates, though. In January 2019, the Charity Commission for England and Wales disqualified three directors of the Cup Trust for 'clear misconduct and mismanagement' in using the charity to operate a tax-avoidance scheme designed to create Gift Aid payments on behalf of its donors. One of the directors received at least £2 million in fees from the operation. Instances like these are hugely damaging for the sector as a whole, since they further dent public confidence into where their donations are going. With charity donations sharply down, *every* penny should be going to the rightful recipients.

Bribery and fraud

In 2018, the NHS Counter Fraud Authority estimated that fraud cost the health service around £1.29 billion per year. This is enough money to pay for over 40,000 staff nurses, or to purchase over 5,000 frontline ambulances. While patient fraud counts for a lot of that figure, with people wrongly claiming for prescriptions and dental fees, a large proportion of that figure is concerned with corruption in the procurement of goods and services. In September 2019, one NHS manager and two contractors were sent to prison and ordered to pay back over £560,000 in costs after a fraud investigation over contracts that were awarded among themselves. Meanwhile, dentists claim around £126 million every year for work on NHS patients that has not been done.

Corruption

Corruption in sport is partly the reason behind why I first decided to write this book. I became so appalled by the FIFA corruption scandal which erupted into the news cycle in 2015, following a raid on a luxury hotel in Zurich and the arrest of seven FIFA executives. At the centre of the unfolding story was the competition to host the World Cup, the most popular sporting event on the globe, which regularly commands TV audiences of more than three billion people. Each time the question of 'where next' comes up, nations vie to attract valuable votes from the committee of FIFA, soccer's ruling body. Now it emerged that some contenders had done quite a bit more than simply marketing the positives of their country as the best place to host the tournament. There were stories of countries horse-trading for votes from the FIFA committee, to straight up paying for them. The decision to award the 2022 World Cup to small, but rich and influential Gulf state of Qatar, which seemed to have a wholly unsuitable climate for hosting the tournament, caused an outcry. However, it was all to no avail, because the World Cup for 2022 is still going to be held in Qatar.

FIFA had made its own earlier investigation into allegations of corruption, and released an executive summary of a report which it said exonerated the bidding process. The report's independent author, American lawyer Michael Garcia, resigned in protest, sparking a series of events that led to an inquiry by the Federal Bureau of Investigation (FBI). Since then, dozens of people have been indicted in a case which involves hundreds of millions of dollars in bribes. Many of the once-untouchable FIFA executives have been banned from the sport, including the long-time president FIFA president, Sepp Blatter. The fact is, though, it would never have come to this if FIFA had been left to investigate itself, as it tried to do.

The new bosses at FIFA have declared a 'new era', condemning what has gone before and moved on as quickly as possible. Even so, there are those that question whether or not such a sweeping corruption case can really be closed so quickly. (At the time of this writing, many of the charges relating to this case have yet to reach the Swiss courts and show no immediate signs of doing so.) It seems reasonable to assume that when a multi-million-dollar enterprise operates without any apparent oversight for so long, the problems will run very deep indeed.

While the FIFA case has been high-profile, it is not the only sporting scandal in recent years. That other great international sporting event, the Olympics, has also been under scrutiny. In this case it was the Winter Olympics, after it emerged that

Russia had been running a systematic campaign of doping its athletes, replying on a complex system of switching urine samples to avoid detection. The subsequent McLaren report, which was commissioned by the World Anti-Doping Agency (WADA), concluded that 1,000 athletes across 30 sports had been assisted by the programme between 2012 and 2015. The spotlight fell on the International Olympic Committee (IOC), who were widely expected to ban Russia from competing in the PyeongChang 2018 Winter Olympics. Except they didn't. At least, not exactly. After dithering for nearly two years, the IOC announced that the Russian team was barred. However, it left open the option for Russian athletes to compete under a neutral flag and wear neutral uniforms. All they needed to do was to prove they were clean and hadn't violated any anti-doping rules. The decision caused another outcry, since the IOC had always made much of its desire for a 'clean sport', yet more than 170 Russians were competing in a very odd fudge of the rules. While a blanket ban would have been tough on clean Russian athletes, it would have sent a clear signal that drugged athletes were not welcome. This was another clear failure of governance, which apparently buckled under the might of Russian pressure.

Price-fixing

The fairness principle underpins free market economies and price-fixing completely undermines this principle. If firms collude, or force unfair prices on consumers, it destroys the positive effects of competition and is ultimately bad for consumers. In 2019, a number of top players in the drug industry, including Teva, Mylan, Novartis Sandoz and Pfizer appeared in US lawsuits after allegations of an anti-competitive conspiracy to artificially inflate prices for more than 100 drugs, some by as much as 1,000%. This came after an earlier case where Pfizer was fined £384 million for ramping up the cost of an epilepsy drug by 2,600%, from £2.83 to £67.50, although the drug maker subsequently won an appeal against the fine. This all has a direct impact in the quality and provision of services to patients. In the hunt for a Covid-19 vaccine, there were widespread fears that pharmaceutical companies would exert too much control over the outcome, effectively deciding who lives and dies.[3]

Mishandling of data

Issues with charities are not simply confined to a lack of oversight or sanctions against individuals who are determined to abuse others. There have also been numerous cases where some of the UK's best-known organisations have pursued a widespread strategy of sharing and even selling the data of millions of their donors, including telephone numbers and email addresses, without their knowledge or consent. Oxfam, Cancer Research UK, the National Society of Prevention of Cruelty to Children, Royal British Legion and WWF-UK were all among the charities fined by the UK's data protection watchdog, the Information Commissioner, in April 2017. The Charities Commission also opened an investigation into a catalogue of failings, including the secret sharing of donor lists with third parties such as lottery companies, passing data to wealth-screening companies to rank the wealthiest donors, and illegally buying information. As well as contravening their rights, the policy undoubtedly caused severe stress and concern to citizens who might, quite rightly, expect these professional organisations to act, well, professionally. The fact that the competition for money and resources is ever greater is no excuse for this sort of behaviour.

Redundancies

The human cost of bad practice in the boardroom cannot be underestimated either. All too often, a scandal will lead onto a reduced head-count in order to recoup costs. In May 2019, students and academics delivered no-confidence votes in University of Surrey vice-chancellor Professor Max Lu. The leadership of the £360,000 a year vice chancellor, who also spent £1,600 of university cash on his dog, came under scrutiny after he told staff that compulsory redundancies could not be ruled out, owing to a shortage of cash. Four out of five students who took part in the vote said they did not believe the performance and leadership of the university governing bodies were satisfactory.

Sexual harassment

One of the biggest scandals of recent times concerns Oxfam after its aid workers were alleged to have used prostitutes in Haiti following the devastating earthquake of 2010 and in Chad in 2006. After the claims were first published, more than 7,000 people cancelled their donations, forcing Oxfam to make £16 million of cuts to its aid projects worldwide. In June 2019, when the Charity Commission published its long-awaited report into the issue, following an 18-month long investigation, it censored Oxfam for a 'culture of tolerating poor behaviour' and its failure to report child abuse claims against its staff.

Sadly, the Oxfam story widened to take in other aid organisations in what has been called a wake-up call for the sector. Save the Children became the subject of another Charity Commission inquiry into its handling of sexual harassment allegations into two senior executives in 2012 and 2015. The charity was subsequently forced to suspend bidding for government funding which would, in turn, have consequences for the children it was set up to protect, since numerous long-term development projects would need to be scaled back. In 2019, Save the Children

announced that as well as a £100 million shortfall in institutional funding, donations from the general public had decreased by £1 million.

Damaged reputation

Entire books could be devoted to the subject of the long-term impact of each of
these scandals on the reputation of the organisations involved, which can be immediate and enduring. Indeed, many have been published on the subject. Yet, it
seems lessons are never learned. Or, perhaps, there are always new scandals to
take their place. There have, for example, been a succession of highly preventable
scandals that seem to bring the shortcomings of NHS management to the top of the
news cycle with alarming frequency. The Alder Hey Children's hospital retained
hundreds of hearts and organs from children without their parents' consent, as well
as 400 foetuses collected from hospitals around the northwest of England. In another case, three nurses at Bridgend's Princess of Wales Hospital were struck off in
2015 after pleading guilty to wilful neglect. They had been falsifying glucose levels
of vulnerable people in the stroke ward because they had been 'too lazy' to check
the readings. In another extreme case, an inquiry found that more than 450 people
had their lives shortened at the Gosport War Memorial hospital between 1987 and
2001. Another 200 were 'probably' given opioids without medical justification in a
case that found a disregard for human life and a culture of shortening the lives of a
large number of patients. In 2010, Dr Jane Barton, who has retired, was found guilty
of multiple instances of professional misconduct by the General Medical Council.
These three instances are all horrifying in their own way and all symptomatic of a
lack of oversight from the top.

—

There have, over the years, been numerous government initiatives to curb corporate
governance abuses. Yet, despite six enquiries, from Cadbury to Walker, the scandals keep occurring. In the past, enquiries have often become too fixated on the
symptoms of the abuses, such as executive pay or length of service, rather than really looking into the crucial role directors play as stewards of their organisations.
There is a tendency for boards to focus on the short-term and monitoring performance rather than really monitoring how they can add long-term value. Although
there are codes advocating a more rigorous selection process for IDs, unfortunately
this does not always happen. While the pandemic undoubtedly encouraged a widespread feeling of goodwill towards our communities, I have no reason to suppose it
will automatically lead to a widespread and enduring adjustment in behaviour.
There is, without a doubt, still a pressing need for further action to improve what
goes on in our boardrooms.

As we have seen from the multitude of scandals details here, spanning a range
of organisations, there is a common theme. Things have become out of control

because the management committees have not heeded important cues about market trends, or internal problems. The consequences are huge and wide-ranging. They impact an organisation's reputation, lead to redundancies, loss of services, and the consequent suffering and disillusionment of millions of people who are affected by these repeated scandals.

Now more than ever, we need to put our organisations on track. We need boards and management committees that will make a real difference. A key component of the action being taken to get our communities back on track should be improving the effectiveness of boards. We need to select the best possible candidates to enhance the performance of board committees. To do this, we need a better pool of qualified, experienced people to put themselves forward.

Notes

1 https://www.moodys.com/research/Moodys-UK-universities-face-increased-financial-pressure-from-rising-staff–PBC_1169029, 4 April 2019.
2 https://inews.co.uk/news/education/university-bankruptcy-reliant-on-loans/, 1 November 2018.
3 https://www.theguardian.com/commentisfree/2020/apr/15/coronavirus-treatment-drug-companies

Chapter 5
Why me? Characteristics of an independent director

Janie Frampton has been passionate about sports from an early age. Her first taste of the prevalence of a fixed mindset about 'boys sports' versus 'girls sports' came as a teenager. Her father was less than impressed to be asked to buy her football boots, when all her brothers were not in the least bit interested in the beautiful game. Janie won that argument and played active sports, whether it was football or athletics, well into her twenties. As time went on, though, she noticed that there seemed to be fewer, not more opportunities. Eventually, stuck for a way to remain involved in women's football, she decided to push things along herself and create an opportunity where none previously existed. She became a referee, coached girls' teams and eventually created a women's league.

As Janie found, rising up the ladder in football was not easy – and certainly not making the transition to the men's game. People flat out asked her: Why do women need to get involved in football? (That may seem a strange question now that England have performed so well in the 2019 Women's Football World Cup.) Undeterred, she became a senior county referee and battled through the frustration of being constantly overlooked to achieve further promotions and to eventually referee pro games.

'I often wonder how I had the strength of character to get through it,' she says. 'Men who were clearly not as well qualified were getting promoted ahead of me. Repeatedly.'

Her persistence won her a role at the Football Association (FA) as one of ten, newly created, regional managers focussed on referee development. At the time, she was one of just five female senior managers in an organisation dominated by men. Despite rising through the organisation to become Head of Referee Development and a consultant on the World Cup, Janie was abruptly sacked in 2012.

The story around the dismissal was extraordinary. Janie's emails were hacked and released to the media. They appeared to offer FA-semi-final tickets in exchange for flight upgrades for three female referees. From the start, there was something very odd about the whole thing and it was pretty clear that someone had been tampering with the emails. Yet, even though there was a hefty data footprint leading to one of Janie's colleagues, an FA internal investigation called for her dismissal. Janie describes an awful four-year period of fighting to clear her name in the face of clear evidence she was not at fault. The lack of support she received was astonishing and shameful. A senior FA employee was eventually convicted and given a suspended sentence for hacking Janie's personal and work email accounts and

https://doi.org/10.1515/9783110706123-005

misusing her data. The FA reached an out of court agreement with Janie after she took them to an employment tribunal to dispute the dismissal.

After being sacked from the FA, Janie started her own business, Sports Officials Consultancy, and also began to take on other roles in sports elsewhere. The roles included becoming an ID on the board of Sports Officials UK, an organisation that supports the educational development of sports officials, and also becoming a member of the English Cricket Board (ECB). She also became a patron for the Muslim Women's Network. Despite the setbacks and lack of support through her career, Janie was determined to make a difference and use her experiences to help others enjoy sport as much as she had always done.

Janie had a wider vision too. She has always believed that sport has the opportunity to have a positive impact on society over and above its role of being entertaining to play and watch. By being more inclusive, it can be a force for good in unifying communities and helping people through times of turmoil. Her view is that there is so much more that can be achieved through the togetherness and camaraderie produced through playing as a team. That is before you even take into account the benefits of getting a wider range of people involved, which in turn has positive impact on health and weight. In Janie's view, her experience with the Muslim Women's Network is a perfect example of this synergy.

'The Muslim Women's Network is a government funded organisation with a 24-hour helpline and I could see many issues coming out from that,' Janie explains. 'As well as incidences of low confidence and self-esteem, there were stories of forced marriage and domestic violence.'

'I thought we could address a lot of these things through sport. We could help women by giving them confidence, so they are able to stick up for themselves. Sport has a role to play in helping people to be stronger members of the community and within their own families.'

In a wide-ranging programme to encourage Muslim women to play support, there have also been initiatives, such as taking nearly 200 Muslim women to see the Women's Cricket World Cup.

Today, Janie says she sees progress being made across the board. She joined the Rugby Football League (RFL) in June 2016, to chair its Match Officials Standards Panel, which is made up of five members, with two of them women. She'd initially been doubtful that she'd get the role, since the main board was predominantly male, but decided to give it a go anyway. After all, the aim of the Match Officials Standards Panel was to examine all the processes around the development and measurement of professional referees. She was awarded the position and has since been working successfully to put in all the processes to grow competencies in the area.

Janie is, not surprisingly, a passionate advocate for more diversity on boards, even if it is not always the easiest path to take. It is, in her view, to the benefit of everyone.

'I think it brings another angle,' she says. 'I'm not saying women are necessarily *better*. We do have a different point of view though and a different set of skills and attributes. We have different levels of emotional intelligence, too. This range of views creates a balance and therefore more rounded and considered decision-making.

'In my experience of all-male boards, there is an arrogance about them. The attitude is that they can weather any storm. In time, whatever it is will blow over. There is no attempt to resolve it and that often doesn't work out so well.'

> If you look back to why things have gone wrong in any organisation, there is always an issue with how effective the board has been. A key element of an ineffective board is having independent directors who are unwilling, or unable, to fulfil their role. When, on the other hand, the independent directors get it right, I am pretty sure that any executive, or shareholder, would acknowledge that they are worth their weight in gold. Independent directors can add a lot of value.
>
> **Mike Clancy, Founder, NED Career Services, Walgrove**

There are no specific qualifications or certifications that a candidate has to have to take an ID role. In fact, theory and education have very little to do with it. There are, however, a range of characteristics and competencies that are essential and count across every sector, regardless of its field of operation. (See Appendix A for a comprehensive list.)

An ID should have a personality which is both engaging and inspiring. Boards and management committees always want to see someone who communicates effectively, but who is as good at listening as they are at talking. When they do speak, what they say should invariably be concise, thoughtful and relevant. A good ID will be calm under pressure, able to manage complex issues and have the ability to see things from another's point of view. It should go without saying that any ID should also have integrity, be honest and have a good ethical and moral compass.

While these qualities are common to all IDs (or should be anyhow), and boards like all-rounders, they are also on the lookout for independent mindsets. We've already looked at the potential to be derived by a diversity of thought. If you are looking for ID roles, you are best advised to show that you'd be very comfortable being objective and focussing on the long-term success of any organisation, even if it means setting aside any personal issues or short-term considerations. IDs need to be relied upon to do the right thing, not the most expedient.

Equally important is the fact there should be ample evidence that a would-be ID is the right fit for the business they want to join. They need to have the right range of skills appropriate to the needs of that organisation at that particular time in its development.

Perhaps one of the most crucial qualities of all, though, is passion about your subject. If you genuinely care about the purpose of the organisation you work for, you will be a formidable ID.

Prospective IDs might like to start thinking about how their previous experience, personal preference, or knowledge of a particular market might be of use by offering a fresh perspective to organisations that operate in their preferred sector. These are the qualities that institutions in this area would be looking for when recruiting an ID. It is becoming increasingly common for boards to recruit on the basis of specific skillsets that are needed to resolve exact challenges faced by that organisation at that particular time. This might, for example, be international expertise, or turnaround experience, or a background in science. There are cases where an organisation will be looking to accelerate growth and will be on the lookout for an ID with a large network of contacts to help make this happen. Schools and universities are very keen on digital right now, so applicants with skills here are most likely to make it to the top of the shortlist. Likewise, almost every sector values applicants who have a financial background, as there will inevitably be posts to fill on the board's audit committee.

Broader requirements to consider include having a good understanding of what governance means in the particular sector being pursued. That means appreciating the legal and regulatory framework that specific organisations work within and the responsibilities and liabilities of directors. As well as reviewing the codes that are in place for that sector (there are governance codes for every sector, all of which are easily found with a Google search), think about it in terms of what good governance looks like and have a clear appreciation of the roles and responsibilities of everyone on the board.

It should be said that not all boards are the same. An obvious statement, I know, but bear with me. The requirements described here are an 'ideal world' scenario, with a professional, well-managed board looking to progress through recruiting IDs with particular expertise. As we have already seen time and time again, not all boards are at this level, even in some of the largest organisations. Sadly, the recruitment criteria may not always be so clear-cut. In some sectors outside the business world, ID job descriptions are not always perfectly well defined. Certainly if, say, you are minded to join the board of a cricket club, you might find that you are surrounded by people who just like playing and watching cricket, rather than experts in the field of raising funds, increasing membership and overseeing the development of a long-term plan. It's not a scenario confined to smaller, regional organisations either.

A colleague who joined the board of a highly rated university was somewhat surprised when he raised the issue of procurement. In his view, the university was a significant commercial entity and could, indeed should, be saving a considerable amount of money on what it was spending each year on goods and services.

'But we're not a business,' came the reply after he raised the issue at a board meeting. 'We're an academic institution.'

To put this into context, this academic institution was spending £400 million a year.

The point here is that it may not always be obvious to every organisation how to improve, even if there is a very real imperative to do so. It may well turn out to be your first task as an ID to persuade your new board that there is a better way. What is most important is that you fully understand what the job is about and then bring your skills to bear.

Risk versus reward

Much has been made of what great value can be derived from an experienced, dedicated ID, as well as the advantages of a more diverse board. You will now also understand more about the skills and personal qualities required to be an effective ID. This is, however, the point where you should pause and think: What is in it for me? The desire to 'make a difference' is laudable, but those three words don't immediately convey the commitment that is involved.

Being an ID is a challenge. In fact, being a good ID involves being a bit of an unsung hero. Indeed, if an organisation is successful, it is often the executives rather than the board who will receive all the plaudits. Meanwhile, if something goes wrong, it is not unusual for the executives to quietly exit stage left, leaving the IDs to pick up the pieces. Without a doubt, you may well be last in the queue for credit and the first in line for blame.

One of the first potential rewards you might consider in the 'what's in it for me' scenario is money. The bad news is that ID roles are not paid nearly as well as you might imagine. In fact, in most cases, there is no compensation at all.

The only ID appointment where you can guarantee payment is in the corporate sector. Here the remuneration will vary according to the size of the organisation, the sector it is in, the time commitment required and the perceived value afforded to that organisation thanks to the ID's ability and experience. The overall package can also be increased by additional fees for serving on board committees. The best rates go to non-executives on the boards of FTSE 100 companies, where the pay ranges from £61,000 to £79,000. The range at FTSE 250 companies falls to between £48,000 and £60,000. With smaller quoted companies, the pay is around £30,000 to £40,000.[1]

There has been much discussion over these pay rates, not least because they have barely changed for some years while the risks and responsibilities that go with the appointments have increased substantially. Those who have challenged the rates as less-than-optimal in relation to the weight of responsibility the job carries, suggest there will be a tipping point in recruitment. This is where the reputational risks become perceived to be so out of proportion with the compensation that it will put off potential new IDs from applying and accepting roles. The opposing argument is that increased pay does not guarantee better performance or governance. As it stands, there is little likelihood of any substantial movement in this direction.

There has been too much criticism in the media and, indeed, via regulators, over the rates of boardroom pay. Many boards believe their hands are tied.

If you believe the corporate rates to be derisory, you will be even more disappointed by rates elsewhere. Those IDs joining boards of small- and medium-sized private companies and NHS Trusts can expect remuneration to begin at around £5,000, but it can be as high as £30,000 per annum.

Anyone beginning in a governor role in a school or college will not receive any payment at all, but will be able to reclaim any reasonable out-of-pocket expenses for travelling to governing body meetings, events or overnight accommodation. At the university level, fees are not paid but again, out of pocket expenses can be claimed.

Trustee roles with charities are also typically unpaid, since you are essentially volunteering your services, although some expenses might be covered. There are some exceptional circumstances where a charity will pay their trustees, but this has to be cleared by the Charity Commission, or the courts. On a positive note, any of these unpaid ID roles can be a useful stepping stone to larger, corporate roles which do bring in an income, if that is your eventual goal.

The clear point to be made here is: Unless you are joining a large, quoted company, money will not be the catalyst for looking for an ID role and therefore cannot be a factor in your decision-making. (Unless the lack of remuneration puts you off the idea entirely.) With this in mind, anyone would be advised to carefully consider what their motivations are for putting themselves in the frame for an ID role, or a number of ID roles.

If the lack of pay and/or recognition hasn't put you off, lets delve more deeply into the questions you are most likely to want answers for before you put yourself forward. In the following section, I have laid out a checklist of questions to consider before pursuing an ID appointment. These questions cover your suitability for ID roles and what it will mean to you on a personal and business level if you choose to try to find one.

What do I have to offer?

If you've had a successful career in senior roles, it's easy to assume that that you have lots to offer a board and that you'll be a shoo-in for the right role. But drill a little deeper into that sentiment. Do you actually have what management committees are looking for? Is this the best, most fitting use of your time and knowledge? This chapter has laid out many of the characteristics required from an ID. How many of them describe you and your experience to date? It can be quite a useful and revealing exercise to review these characteristics and match them to your own strengths. It's not a wasted exercise either, since much of this can be used for your CV and in the networking and application process to come.

Not all boards will be looking for someone with previous executive experience in the boardroom, as they would if you were applying for a position on the board of a large, listed corporation. What is important for any organisation you hope to join will be a basic understanding of finance. You should be comfortable with a profit and loss sheet. While you won't be compiling the accounts, one of your roles will be to scrutinise the accounts and you need to be able to understand whether or not the organisation is delivering on the bottom line. A general lack of financial expertise among many board teams has been cited as a contributing factor to many past scandals, when strategies were waved through on the nod, simply because some IDs did not understand the full picture. Obviously, the depth of financial knowledge required will vary according to the size and authority of the management committee you hope to join. Certainly though, for effective decisions to be made on any board, there needs to be a good understanding of finance.

There is much more of a requirement for functional expertise today. Nearly every ID job description will have a need for specific desired qualities. If you have a bedrock skill in HR, or sales and marketing, that will bode well. In addition, frequently there is demand for expertise in mergers and acquisitions, or international experience.

Technology skills, in particular, are at a premium today. The internet is having a profound effect on all areas of activity around the globe, from commerce to recreation, to health and sport. Many organisations have just about managed to keep up with developments such as mobile networks, the internet and video, but find themselves scrabbling to adapt to the never-ending flood of new developments such as material sciences, AI and biotechnology. While there is a general acknowledgement that these innovations will have a profound effect, there are few people that properly understand how, or even how to best incorporate them into their particular circumstance to gain an edge. This is why anyone who has up-to-date tech know-how will find their services valued at a premium almost everywhere.

When I met the chief digital officer of Exeter, I made it clear that if I thought that we weren't going to get on, then I wouldn't have taken the role. There's no point banging your head against a brick wall throughout your tenure. I was also very frank with Sarah (Turvill, chair of council, University of Exeter) when we met and asked, 'Is Exeter up for transformation? Is it up for investing in it?' The fact that she and the vice chancellor were enthusiastic meant that at least I felt I had a sympathetic audience. The results would flow from that.

The relationship I had with the execs at Exeter was strong, because I invested my reputation, as well as my time, in advocating for the thing that they were working towards. That didn't mean that I was unable or unwilling to provide challenge. However, they knew I had their back, and they knew I understood at least as much as they did about the strategic direction and the challenges that they were experiencing.

There were advantages for my career, too. I'm still relatively early on in my non-exec career. I wanted to learn from the operation of the board as a whole, and also from the input of Sarah as chair of the board. There was also a big element of just caring about higher education and the strength and success of organizations like Exeter and how they can be the best they can be. I don't mean to be like a Victorian backwater of pedagogy from the previous century, but to be able to use all of the advances in technology that we can now capitalize upon in the pursuit of better education, better teaching, better learning, better assessment, better research and better administration.

Richard Sargeant, Chief Commercial Officer, Faculty; ID, Exeter University;
Government Centre for Data Ethics and innovation

It should also be said that, just as having a basic understanding of finance is increasingly important, the same goes for embracing technology. Everyone applying for an ID role should have a certain level of technological competence. IDs certainly need to understand the impact of social media (good and bad), the 24-hour news cycle, e-commerce, ever-more interconnected markets and other mobile technologies. All of these developments have irrevocably changed the way consumers react with brands and can drive organisations in entirely different trajectories. On a purely practical basis, IDs need to be comfortable with the digital dissemination of information, which occurs on a 24–7 basis. The ability to react to events at a time of your own choosing is long gone.

Something else that is more of a requirement today is an understanding of risk. As per the previous chapter, there is an increased scrutiny of scandals affecting organisations of all sizes and sectors, and a will to stop them before they start. That begins in the boardroom and means there is a greater onus on IDs to fully understand all forms of risky behaviour, be it operational, financial or reputational. This is not simply in terms of identifying *obvious* potential problems, but also to be able to think the unthinkable to ensure nothing slips through because the full implications are not fully explored. There needs to be a will to ask difficult questions and to press the point home when required.

It may help to list a few undesirables when it comes to what boardrooms are or are not looking for. First and foremost, those with big egos who adore grandstanding are never a good fit. Likewise, anyone who envisages using the platform to promote their own agenda, whether it is a drive for greater political correctness, diversity or corporate social responsibility. These are all laudable aims, but the starting position is the board itself and the priorities for the organisation it serves. The rest comes later. IDs are there to represent shareholder interests, not their own.

While any ID should absolutely be able to hold their own, individuals who are confrontational or controversial for the sake of it will make poor IDs. Anyone who tends to stick to an argument through thick and thin, regardless of the evidence presented, will also find boardrooms an unsatisfactory environment. The feeling will no doubt be echoed by their committee colleagues. Equally important, there needs to be full commitment to the job of ID. This means that individuals need to mentally sign up for spending time perusing board materials, as well as going to meetings and possibly attending committees. If they are unable to do so, it is a waste of everyone's time and is also hugely frustrating for other board members who do put in the effort. Finally, there needs to be a clear understanding of the ID role and, in particular, its distinction from the executive one. IDs should not be focussed on showing off their leadership, or strategic know-how. Nor are they expected to shoulder the task of operational decision-making. It's not just a question of not treading on any toes: this approach will seriously undermine the smooth running of the board and could well end in conflict and chaos.

How will I find the right board?

The 'right' role for you is one which is not just a good fit with your skills and experience, but also complements your culture and values. This will have a great bearing on your view of the experience. While diversity is an asset, since it guarantees a broad range of opinions, you should be wary of joining a board which does not align with your values. It will inevitably lead to conflict which is not only frustrating, but also not very productive.

Most of all, it is important that the board in question genuinely excites you and makes you feel that you can make a notable difference. This will ensure that you not only make a positive contribution, but that you also find the experience personally rewarding.

A good starting point is to consider what it is that you are passionate about. Have you been personally affected by funding cuts in the health service, either during the pandemic or previously? Or, have you been inspired by Greta Thunberg, the teenage environmental activist, who has carried her campaign to raise global awareness of climate change all the way from Sweden to the White House, by boat? Or, is there an issue closer to home, in your local community which appears to be spiralling out of control? You may well have donated in the past, or attended fundraisers, or perhaps know others in the community who are involved with a charity. Imagine how much more your active input could help these organisations that directly serve your community. By serving on the board, you'll be able to use your understanding of what the organisation does and how much it means to those around it, in order to make your contribution so much more effective.

Some people choose to start at places with which they share an interest. If, say, you have close links with your local sports club, you can rest assured that if you volunteer to sit on their governing bodies, you'll be connecting with others who are as passionate and committed about the sport as you. Together you'll be able to help foster the improvements you may have long grumbled about being needed. Along the way, you'll most likely learn a lot from your fellow sports club members and gain valuable insights into the sport. Equally important, you'll enjoy the experience, too.

Alternatively, those with an interest in the education system might be interested in exploring the options for becoming a school governor, or to sit on the boards of further education establishments. There is a huge sense of satisfaction to be derived from the knowledge that the next generation will directly benefit from your efforts. It's also an opportunity to work with a wide range of people from a variety of social, cultural and religious backgrounds. Plus, as well as working with fellow parents, it is, of course, an opportunity to make a real positive impact on your local area.

Any of these could be your starting point. If you have firm views on any sector – whether it is business, sport, health, charity or education, or indeed any other area of your business or personal life – this is your opportunity and your inspiration to make a difference. In each case, it is more than possible to hold a full-time job while actively contributing to the community.

> If you have some sort of emotional connection, whether it is through geography, or you have had some prior association or close link with an institution, it is very important. When you are passionate about a sector, you'll be motivated to actively do something. There are some business and sectors that I am not very interested in and know very little about. There would be no point in me joining their board.
>
> **Richard Atkins, Further Education Commissioner for England and Independent Member, Exeter University Council**

How much due diligence should I do?

A lot. While competition for the most coveted roles can be fierce, it is inadvisable to leap into the first position you are offered. An independent directorship is a complex role with clear expectations of competence, ethics and behaviours. All directors, regardless of their experience, are bound by strict regulations and legislations. Most sectors have their own strict codes, too. Legal liability begins from day one, even if it takes you a while to get up-to-speed with what might be a very different role. Pause for a moment to think about this. Even though you are with an organisation for, say, two or three days a month as an ID, you have the same potential liabilities as a full-time executive. You will be putting your reputation and more on the line. It can be a very different role, legally, psychologically and strategically, from any of your previous positions.

Those who join boards, either as executives or IDs, are often surprised by the complexity and scope of what is involved. There are a number of elements to take into account over and above having a general overview of an organisation's operational activities and corporate governance, including understanding the exposure to risk and strategic direction. You need to fully understand the organisation you are considering joining, its history, its goals and how it has responded to challenges in its sector. Do thorough research into the background and experience of others on the board as part of your due diligence.

This process will not end once a board position is offered and accepted. IDs are advised to continue the process of developing their understanding of the organisation and its role in the wider sector, as well as building relationships with key individuals. (Further information on the scope of due diligence is found in Chapter 6.)

Do I have the time?

At one time, the ID role was firmly linked with retirees who had completed a successful executive career and then took on one or a handful of positions to see them through their later years as a modest distraction. This might have been because they wanted to give something back to their sector, or perhaps keep their mind, body and soul active after leaving full-time work. This is possibly how the role came to be seen as a 'softer' option. Fortunately, this vision is now much less prevalent, thanks to stringent demands placed on directors by regulators. The quality of boards has markedly improved and an ID role is (fortunately) beginning to become synonymous with taking up a vital and challenging job which needs to be taken very seriously. Depending on the position you take, it can require much more than a handful of days per year to be effective.

The most challenging option, timewise, is for IDs who take on their first role while still working full-time in their day job. As discussed in Chapter 2, this means gaining permission from the chairperson and CEO at the business where you are contracted full-time. As well as being fully committed to the benefits of CSR, your bosses will also need to be convinced of the fact that there are no conflicts of interest in the role you are seeking. Naturally, it should not detract from the job you are paid to do either. Ideally, it should be complementary. This also applies if you are currently out of work and seeking a new full-time position. If you take on an ID role as a stop-gap to further your skills, how will it impact your 'saleability' to a new employer? It might be seen as a good thing, but equally, some employers might not see the advantages or be willing to accommodate it.

My role at Plymouth Argyle is a bit of an ice breaker where I work at University of Exeter. A lot of people there are well into their football and will stop me on campus to talk about it. It's good to have something different to share with them. It's also made me think more closely about the subject of membership and what it means to be a fan. How do we, as an organisation, treat people who are our fans and have certain expectations? In a university context, our alumni are almost the equivalent of fans, while the students and academics are our players. The alumni fan base supports us from the touch lines. It's crucial to keep them up to date with what is going on and to properly respect that relationship. Just as in football clubs, football managers and players come and go, but the fans always stay loyal. It's the same with universities. You are an alumnus at a university all your life.

There are other parallels too. One of the biggest challenges for universities right now is recruiting boys from a working-class background. Where do these boys go? They go to the football. This is why quite a few universities are involved in sponsorships with football clubs.

> My involvement with Plymouth provokes a different way of thinking about how things work.
>
> **Jane Chafer, Various ID Positions Including Plymouth Argyle,**
> **Sheffield International Venues, FX Plus**

The best-case scenario is where an employer is convinced that taking up such a role will make a real difference to their employees' personal development which will, in turn, feed back into their performance with their main employer. The most ideal situation is one where your employer has links with the organisation which you want to join as an ID. An engineering firm might, for example, have links with a local technical college. It would make perfect sense to cement that link by allowing one of its senior employees to join the technical college board. The benefits would run both ways: motivating, enabling and developing that team member by broadening their working day, while at the same time ensuring the link is being run properly and is beneficial to all parties.

An ID appointment can also be seen as an important part of a strategy to retain key members of any team. There are, after all, a finite number of board-level roles in any business. Only a handful of senior executives in any organisation will make it to the main board, so flexibility in allowing people to gain ID experience elsewhere is a good way to ensure continued engagement. In addition, it is also a useful filter to see who has the capability to rise to a main board role. However, don't assume you will have the green light. It is always important to clear this upfront.

Something that also needs to be agreed upon is how many days you, as a contracted employee, will be allowed to devote to any ID position and how these days will be accounted for. Will the prospective ID take all the time needed as unpaid leave, or will they be using holiday entitlement, or will their firm will allow them to do it on their time, or a combination of all of these? Some employers will allocate their staff a certain amount of days off for voluntary roles, and the rest of the time required will have to be taken as part of their usual holiday entitlement. Even if an employer is supportive, though, it can still be quite a tough juggling act, even for the most experienced executive.

What is the time commitment?

The amount of commitment and time that is needed to devote to an ID role can vary from organisation to organisation and also the type of ID role being undertaken. The 2009 Walker Review recommended a minimum expected time commitment of thirty to thirty-six days a year for IDs working for financial institutions, but this is for paid ID roles. Elsewhere, in corporate roles for large organisations, between 23 to 31 days in a year is the norm according to research from MM&K.[2] However, with smaller voluntary organisations, there is considerably less time commitment.

School governors may only be required for one meeting a term, while anyone joining a University Council will be needed for a few days a month. Similarly, anyone applying to sit on an NHS Trust should expect to devote at least two or three days a month to the task. Depending on the severity of the problems facing the individual trust, it may be necessary to spend many more days. For charity trustee roles, the time commitment will vary according to the size of the charity. The larger the charity, the more days trustees will be expected to attend. Bear in mind, if your main employer runs an ESV scheme, or is open to starting one, your corporate volunteering could, in the main, be done in work time. You may only need to take one or two days of holiday a year to cover the time, or indeed, might not need to do so at all, if the committee timetable is work-friendly, which it often is.

The workload in any management committee can be sporadic. The role might be advertised as two days a month, but you may very well find yourself working intensely for longer one month in order to respond to a specific circumstance and then barely at all for the following four months. Meanwhile, you will be expected to be 'on call' should a situation arise.

It is, however, worth noting that over and above the sporadic nature of the position, IDs often report that these roles require more time overall than they originally anticipated when they first took them on. There is, for example, frequently a great deal of background reading that needs to be done, occasional fact-finding visits to individual sites of operations, and time spent speaking to other stakeholders. These are all crucial aspects of the role that need to be factored into the timetable over and above regular board meetings. IDs who sit on specialist committees (see Chapter 6) must also be prepared to spend even more time in the role.

It should also be noted that the time spent within an organisation as an ID, is very different to spending time there as an employee, however senior. You may be there just one or two days a month, but in that brief time, you need to be right on it, wide awake and energised. People who are in an office day-after-day have the luxury of time to establish a rapport with colleagues and get to the bottom of what is going on. They can take half an hour to walk the floor a bit. It's much tougher to build chemistry and a productive relationship on a part-time basis.

Can I contribute?

Being an effective ID boils down to behaviour and the way you engage your fellow board members. After all, you can have all the skills and knowledge in the world, but it is how you deploy them that counts. If the rest of the board ignore what you have to say, then you will not get very far.

One of the first things to remember is: you're not there to run the organisation. You are there to make sure that it is run properly. This can be quite a tough balancing act to get it right, particularly for those who hail from an executive background.

Executives generally operate in a command and control structure. They are used to having power and making decisions based on the available knowledge and telling people what to do. Being an ID is 180 degrees different. Here, the way to get on is to suggest and influence behaviour. Any ID who swaggers into a management committee and throws their weight about declaring that 'this is the way to do it', will either get pretty short shrift, or be ignored altogether.

The reason for the differences in approach required are quite fundamental. In an executive position, there are certain levers to pull. Anyone running a team wields power because they can issue a number of sanctions if subordinates don't fall into line and fulfil what they have been asked to do. They can give them a poor appraisal, overlook them for promotion, or side-line them from an important project. As an ID, there are very few levers to pull if the rest of the board is not aligning with your viewpoint. In fact, in my opinion there is only one. Indeed, I will often articulate it to the chief executive when I first start working as an ID:

> 'You have my unconditional support right up until the day that you give me reason that I have to fire you.'

It's a blunt message, told in a light-hearted way, but ultimately this is the only sanction an ID has. Clearly it can't be used too often, so that means the only way to make things happen is to persuade and influence. It's a collaboration, not a competition.

Will I learn?

When the Plymouth Argyle opportunity came up, I was also offered another ID role at the same time. I spoke to work and they said: *You have a full-time job here, so you can only really do one. You've got to choose.* I chose the football one, because it was going to be unlike anything I had ever done before. I knew it would take me out of my comfort zone in terms of what they were dealing with and the kind of people I would meet. I also really liked the fact that it was part of the fabric of the city. It was never going to be a boring post, with dry papers and dry meetings. It would be fascinating, fantastic and emotional. That was a big draw.

Jane Chafer, Various ID Positions Including Plymouth Argyle, Sheffield International Venues, FX Plus

Another of the advantages of working on a diverse board is that your fellow directors will most likely be from entirely different backgrounds. You might meet lawyers, engineers, entrepreneurs, seasoned CEOs – anything, really. All of you will be working together closely on the same board. It's a great opportunity to listen and learn, building on your own skillsets by closely observing others from entirely different trades. It's a two-way process, too. You will be sharing your own expertise with this group. The more you help others learn and develop, the more influential you become as the go-to person in your particular area. This is an important part of building up the relationships that you'll need to get things done.

In addition, feedback has become an important part of the board remit. Board reviews/evaluation have been introduced and they put an increased emphasis on contribution and performance. Many boards and management committees are voluntarily subjecting themselves to peer reviews, and IDs are increasingly receiving detailed expert advice on ways they might be able to have more impact in the boardroom. The emphasis is very much on a continual learning process, which is hugely beneficial for anyone looking for ongoing personal development.

If you have chosen to take on an ID role while still working full-time elsewhere, this can be a very valuable learning opportunity indeed. You will not only be gaining useful experience into how an ID operates, which will come in handy if you decide to expand your ID portfolio later on, but you'll also be gaining useful insight that can be used back in your 'day job'. Even if you are already in a senior executive role, there's the chance to see things from another perspective. You'll develop a more holistic view of how different organisations work as a whole and gain valuable insights into the impact of various teams. It may well stimulate you into asking more pertinent questions to get better results in your existing organisation.

> It is a great way to develop executives and to let them see how things work in a different environment. It challenges your thinking and the conventional wisdom about doing things in one way simply because they have always been done in that way.
>
> **Ruth Cairnie, Chair Babcock International, Non-Executive Rolls Royce, Associated British Foods and ContourGlobal**

Will it be fun?

A key driver for any ID is that they fundamentally enjoy business and management. They enjoy mixing with other like-minded people and spending time solving problems. This is a great opportunity to build on that interest.

Should I expect a board induction?

In the corporate world, it's best practice that all newly appointed IDs should receive a comprehensive, tailored induction programme. The objective is to provide a new director with all the information that he or she requires in order to become as effective as possible in their role in the shortest possible time. The 2003 Higgs Suggestions for Good Practice stated that the induction process should aim to achieve the following three things:

– Build an understanding of the nature of the company, its business and its markets
– Build a link with the company's people
– Build an understanding of the company's main relationships

Input into this process should be both ways and there should be ongoing training as and when required.

There are no guarantees that all the ID positions being discussed here will have a formal induction process. Indeed, with many of the smaller organisations, it is quite unlikely to be the case. If there is not an induction process, it is advisable to construct one of your own just so you can understand the committee a little better before you start. Certainly, it would be good to spend a day with senior management, getting to understand everyone's roles and a little about them as people. Ask for the last one or two board packs to go over too. More information about the induction process is contained in Chapter 9.

One thing that hasn't been specifically included in this list is your personal situation. I will touch upon it now because it is something that is well worth giving some thought to, before going too much further. If you are considering becoming an ID, you will most likely need some sort of home office set-up, because it's quite likely that this will become your centre of operations. You can't, after all, use work time in your main job to get up to speed with ID paperwork. That would push your employer's tolerance to the limits, even if they are fully behind you and running a comprehensive ESV programme.

Many people do now have efficient home office set-ups, thanks to the enforced period of homeworking during the pandemic. Even so, on a purely practical level, ask yourself whether your home is the right environment to run your new ID career. It is quite possible that you may need to spend some time on the phone speaking with fellow committee members or working on ID business. That constantly barking dog next door might prove to be a problem. You'll also need to think about IT. With so much of our lives run online today, you will need the capacity (and good enough broadband) to be able to communicate effectively online via video conferencing or Skype. Little things make all the difference. What, for example, would your interlocutor be looking at in the background of your home office when you speak via Skype? Again, though, these are problems you will have already ironed out.

Organising a parallel career as an ID is not always easy, with meetings to attend and papers to read. There is a great deal of commitment and engagement required of a modern-day ID. There are rewards, though, in terms of an enjoyable, learning experience where you will be giving something back to your chosen area.

Notes

1 IoD Business Information Services, Life in the Boardroom, NED pay survey.
2 https://mm-k.com

Chapter 6
What will you be signing up for?

Curiosity is a crucial ingredient when it comes to being an independent director. You will receive a great deal of information from management, whether it is a report on recent performance, a proposal or a discussion document on new strategy. It is inevitable that you will always have a lot less information than management, though. It is up to you to be curious and inquire, and then distil out, so you can get to the bottom of what the important things are to talk about.

Ruth Cairnie, Chair, Babcock International, Non-Executive Rolls Royce, Associated British Foods and ContourGlobal

Whether they are at the head of a FTSE 100 blue chip corporation, an NHS Trust, or a university, boards have a huge role to play. In businesses, they are responsible for delivering shareholder value and maintaining the long-term health of the company. In an educational or sporting context, boards develop and approve an institution's long-term mission, strategic goals and objectives, to improve the lives of people that use their services. Meanwhile, charitable and hospital boards are the guardians of purpose, making sure that all decisions in that organisation put the intended beneficiaries first.

To achieve their main objectives, all boards and management committees must fulfil a broad (and growing) range of requirements which take into account all of their stakeholders, as well as an array of ethical and governance issues. Boards routinely face a vast range of decisions. Here is just a small sample of what might be concentrating minds in the board room at any one time:

- What companies/countries should they do business with and what is the standard of ethics and governance at those companies/countries?
- Are schemes to minimise tax and maximise earnings prudent, or a potential PR minefield?
- What will the perception of executive pay and stock options be among shareholders/the public?
- What are the long-term implications of increasing the customer base via price fixing, price exploitation or dumping?
- How safe are the organisation's products or services?
- Will environmental policies meet heightened global awareness/concerns on climate change?

As I said, this is just a small sample of a long list of possibilities. The point to remember is that a board has a large, wide-ranging remit.

Boards largely follow the same format of a mix of executive and non-executives, or IDs, who need to work closely and collaboratively in order to succeed. The individuals may have slightly different titles, though. In the charity

https://doi.org/10.1515/9783110706123-006

sector, for example, all members of the board of charity trustees – including where they are directors of the charity – will be volunteers, so they could theoretically be called non-executive or independent directors. However, this belies the fact that, in some cases, individuals will be on the board by virtue of their paid role in the charity or another capacity such as marketing, or fundraising. Similarly, in the university sector, a large number of university councils are 'lay' members, external to the university. This is the case with my own role at Exeter University, which is very similar to a corporate non-executive role. The other members on a university council will be university staff, in both academic and support roles.

What is important to note here is that the executive members and IDs have a very different remit. Executive directors have executive responsibility for *running* an organisation. In a corporate setting, they are company employees, usually a senior executive and a board member, on top of their full-time executive position. Three of the most common executive positions generally found on a board are CEO, managing director and CFO. The appointment of executives is typically made by a nominations committee (see the section on board committees).

IDs are often *employed* by an organisation, and *appointed* via a letter of appointment. Their role is to challenge, question and monitor the CEO and senior management and bring an independent perspective to decision-making.

To further explain how the roles of executives and IDs differ, it's helpful to go through some of the key responsibilities of a board and discuss the respective roles.

Strategic direction

At its simplest level, the purpose of board and management committees is to be collectively responsible for the long-term success of an organisation, balancing the interests of all its stakeholders by overseeing and directing its activities. In the UK, it is common for the executive board to be directly involved in setting and championing strategy, which is presented to the board. Then, once it has been adopted, they will monitor it over time to make sure it is correctly executed.

When discussing the strategic options presented to the board, it is the job of the independent director to ensure *all* stakeholders are considered, whether it is employees, customers, the community, or society at large. Ultimately, they need to be able to robustly counter any criticism that any strategy being adopted apparently prioritises shareholders above all else, or indeed any another specific group who will gain an advantage, generally financially. This requires IDs to take a wider view of the external factors affecting the company and its environment. Think of it as standing back and viewing an organisation and its activities with the critical eye of an outsider. As constructive critics, IDs look at the objectives and plans devised by the chief executive and the executive team, and judge the optics from the point of view of everyone who might be affected.

Monitor performance

In respect of strategy, as outlined in the previous section, it is the ID's role to take responsibility for monitoring the progress and performance of the executive team in meeting the agreed goals.

While an ID will inevitably build up good working relationships with others on the board, they must not fall into the trap of going with the flow and going along with everything being said. Their duty is *not* to the executive team, and executives can't be allowed to mark their own homework.

It's not always an easy balancing act to pull off. It takes tact, diplomacy and courage. The penalties for not achieving this delicate balance are high, as we saw in Chapter 4. IDs that fail to rein in overbearing executives often find themselves embroiled in very public scandals later on. In this case, there isn't just bad publicity to fear, either. Increasingly, IDs are finding themselves in line for prosecution if the company breaches the law.

Succession planning

The board is also responsible for ensuring it is composed of the best possible people for the job, which also falls squarely within the remit of directing the long-term success of an organisation. Succession planning is crucial so that there are people in place to carry on the work of key individuals should they leave the company, either in a planned manner – such as through retirement or a job move – or in an unplanned manner, such as an unexpected removal from post. Ideally, an immediate successor will be there and waiting; a safe pair of hands, ready to carry on the work. Top performing firms are often characterised by the fact they manage this succession well. When I was an ID on the board at Forth Ports, for example, the chairman Chris Collins gave us two years notice that he was intending to step down. This made all the difference when it came to finding the right successor. No organisation wants to be in a position of a last-minute scramble to find appropriate senior executives.

One of the most crucial roles to plan for is a change of CEO. There are two options here. The first is where organisations develop and promote the next in line from within. This can be a time-consuming process and candidates will often require the benefit of a lengthy mentoring and grooming process to prepare them for the job. Alternatively, an outside recruit can be brought in. This presents its own challenges, since the new appointment needs to be able to fit in quickly, have a full understanding and empathy for the culture and values of the organisation, as well as for its strategy and stakeholder expectations.

According to the UK Corporate Governance Code (2016), this is all within the remit of IDs who have 'a prime role in appointing and, where necessary, removing executive directors, and in succession planning.' IDs should also be satisfied that plans are in place for an orderly succession of appointments to the board and to the senior management team. These appointments need to maintain an appropriate balance of skills and experience in the organisation.

The process for succession is led by a nominations committee and there is more information about this later in this chapter.

Audit and compliance

It is the duty of the whole board to ensure an organisation fulfils its legal and financial responsibilities. This includes the auditing of accounts and their presentation to shareholders as a true and fair reflection of the activities carried out.

Once again, IDs have a key role to play here via the audit committee and this is described in greater detail in the next section. IDs also undertake joint responsibility for legal compliance, ethics, and health and safety. These are crucial elements of any board role, since any mistakes could land an organisation in legal hot water, or worse. Many high-profile safety failures over recent years have been rooted in failures of leadership. BP is a prime example with two high-profile examples in recent memory. The Texas City Refinery explosion in March 2005 killed 15 workers and injured 180 others. In the subsequent enquiries, both BP and the US Chemical Safety and Hazard Investigation Board identified numerous technical and organisational failings, both at the refinery and within corporate BP. Following the Deepwater Horizon explosion in 2010 that killed 11 crewmen and which led to the largest ever oil spill in US waters, BP was found guilty of gross negligence and wilful misconduct. The fine ran into many billions.

For boards that neglect their duties when it comes to health and safety, the stakes are getting higher, too. The Corporate Manslaughter and Corporate Homicide Act 2007 introduced a specific offence for killing for the first time. Organisations face an unlimited fine if they are found guilty of causing a death if the way their activities are managed amount to a gross breach of its duty of care.

Remuneration and reward

Pay and rewards require a great deal of informed judgement, whatever the organisation. Money is always an emotive subject, and providing people with the right level of compensation while also protecting the financial interests of the organisation they work for is a difficult balancing act to get right – very much more so in the present economic climate. The difficulties of this delicate task can be compounded if an organisation is facing financial constraints, which is frequently the case in the public sector but again is more likely further afield today. IDs are responsible for determining the appropriate levels of remuneration via the remuneration committee.

Risk management

Understanding the risks involved with running an organisation is a crucial, yet often underestimated role. While many executives and IDs are focused on dealing with opportunities, there is not always a similar level of confidence when it comes to the understanding and management of risks. According to one McKinsey survey, while 'boards are taking more responsibility for strategy, risk management is still a weak spot – perhaps because boards (and companies) are increasingly complacent about risks, as we move further out from the 2008 financial crisis.'[1] Once more, these comments were made ahead of the pandemic and we have yet to see the full effects of the precipitous drop in the markets as a result of the health crisis.

Executives and IDs both need a clear oversight of the key risks involved with the delivery of their organisation's objectives. To aid their decision-making, they need to understand the levels of risk that are acceptable, and the controls that are available. Let's take an example which is pertinent to many organisations today: IT. In any organisation that has been around for any length of time, it is quite likely that their IT systems have not kept pace with either the growth of that organisation, or its day-to-day requirements, or the latest tech available. It's not uncommon for new IT to be bolted on to existing systems, in a sticking plaster-style approach, to keep everything running as smoothly as possible. Sooner or later, a discussion needs to be had about whether to completely overhaul or upgrade the creaking IT system. Some board members might see no value in doing so, or may not believe that the investment is warranted. Others might judge that sticking with the status quo presents risks to the support and continuity of business. What is needed here is a clear understanding of the risks of any proposed solution. After all, a complete overhaul may resolve some risks, but present other new ones. You may well remember the catastrophic IT meltdown at the TSB in 2018, which resulted in 12,500 customers subsequently closing their accounts out of sheer frustration. The bank had been attempting to move from a legacy IT system installed by its previous owner Lloyds Banking Group, to a new one run by its current parent company Sabadell. In the resulting software failure, two million people, or more than a third of TSB's 5.2 million customers, experienced problems with mobile and online payments. To make matters worse, fraudsters took advantage of the situation and stole money from 1,300 customers, many of whom lost their entire life savings. In the enquiries that followed, TSB which had by this time earned the unedifying epithet of 'Truly Shambolic Bank', found itself being accused of being 'over-optimistic' about the switch. This is not a situation any board would ever want to find itself in. A clear understanding of any risks is crucial.

The benefits of good risk management go beyond avoiding a disaster like that which struck TSB. They include:

– Improved predictability of results against forecasts and plans. This is important so stakeholders can count on management to deliver what they promise.

- Fewer unwanted surprises. Unseen or unplanned for incidents have a very negative impact on any brand's reputation. They also call into question the integrity of management.
- Improved compliance with laws and regulations. This is a crucial duty of board members. Get it wrong and there is the risk of investigation, falling foul of regulators, spiralling legal costs and maximum reputational damage, not to mention potential prosecution.
- Enhanced brand and reputation. This works both ways. An organisation that routinely delivers and has a consistent and long-term performance will inevitably earn the respect and loyalty of stakeholders.

Once again, the need for a range of different options and points of view is vital in shaping board discussions and analysis of potential risks in order to make the right choice.

Communication

A key part of the ID role is to exercise accountability to all relevant stakeholders, which makes communication an important part of the job. This entails a complete understanding of the range of interests of those stakeholders and then ensuring that these needs are responded to in an effective way. There will, of course, be an element of managing expectations. You can't, as they say, please all of the people, all of the time. The way to do this is to explain, rather than avoid, and to be as transparent as possible within the realms of commercial confidentiality and legal restrictions.

Stakeholders need to be appraised of a wide range of issues, concerning everything on the list featured here, such as levels of risk, remuneration, compliance and strategy. Often, this will require instigating a dialogue to discuss certain actions. Boards are often criticised for being too far removed from what is going on daily. Therefore, I would recommend that any ID takes efforts to be seen and to be visible so that people can talk to them about their concerns. Clearly, IDs can certainly discuss confidential matters, and being seen to take an interest and giving out what information they can could make a huge difference. Where there are opportunities to put things right, they should make all efforts to do so.

Keeping in touch with all relevant stakeholders can often take some doing, particularly for IDs of international companies. Certainly, when I was an ID at Keller, I made time to visit subsidiaries abroad and would travel to at least two a year. While with Quintiles Transnational Corporation, my schedule was even more active. I visited up to a dozen countries a year, taking in sites belonging to the global leader in clinical development and commercial outsourcing services to the biopharmaceuticals industry. I always made a point of attending a dinner with key staff the day before any formal meetings at each office. The reason I did this was to keep the lines of communication open and because I wanted to get to know key staff and better understand business issues. However, I was always very aware that while it can be a worthwhile experience in gaining greater insight into decision-making and in contributing valuable expertise, there is a balance to be had.

Something that needs to be considered today is the use of social media, which can be a potent communication tool when used in the right way. It can also be employed in a very detrimental and damaging way. One thing that all IDs need to get used to is seeing abusive messages online about their organisation or key executives, particularly at a time when people feel vulnerable and emotions are running high. This is particularly common in a public-facing organisation such as university, where people won't hold back if they disapprove of what the vice chancellor is doing. IDs can't engage with this dialogue. The best they can do is to ensure their organisation puts out clear approved statements, and that communication between it and the stakeholders making the allegations (unfounded or otherwise) provides as much information as possible in order to clear up any misunderstanding or unrest. If IDs do use digital media in any way, they should always be sure to do so in a professional manner.

Due diligence

In the case of any acquisition, whether the organisation in question is buying another one, or being taken over itself, the whole board should be involved. There will certainly be a requirement for IDs to play a role in due diligence. This will include scrutinising valuations and giving consideration to the strategic importance and value of any acquisition. If the intention is to merge two organisations, analysis will be needed on the competencies of the management team on the other side, as well as of any broader issues that might arise through the integration.

The evolution of the ID role means that in each of these cases, their responsibilities go far beyond that of merely saying yes to whatever the chief executive directs. The onus is on IDs to have a deep understanding of the details and any decisions being made, and to challenge anything they don't feel comfortable with. This involves having open and thorough conversations with everyone on the board.

The increased intensity of the role does provoke a debate about how far IDs need to go beyond the original job description. As previously discussed, we have moved away from the stage where an ID simply turned up to a meeting once every month or so. To keep on top of a role like this, it may require two or three days a month. IDs may attend strategy days when the senior team meets off-site, perhaps once or twice a year. Some IDs feel it is necessary to attend internal meetings relevant to any particular committee they sit on, including spending time with divisional finance directors.

Board committees

> Boards really do try to bring their best people onto committees. It can be a very powerful position, though. If, say, the audit committee feels that something has not gone right, they can demand a report and question it. On remuneration, we rely on a lot of outside data to make sure we pitch it just right. It can add substantially to the time commitment. The committees meet three or four times a year, but there is also a lot of paperwork to go through ahead of the meetings. It can take at least a day before each meeting.
>
> **Sarah Turvill, Chair of Council, University of Exeter**

The idea behind board committees is that they can take care of specific tasks for which the board is responsible. By delegating these tasks to committees, the board is able to spend the rest of its time dealing with other matters more efficiently. It is not always mandatory to have board committees, particularly in companies that are not listed in the stock market, but many governance codes recommend it as best practice to include certain key committees.

The type of committees each board has will depend very much on the nature of the organisation and its size, as well as the recommendations from the relevant code. The two most high-profile committees that can be found in pretty much any organisation are those responsible for remuneration and audit. You might also find committees for a nomination, health and safety and quality. Companies in the financial services sector also have ethics and risks committees.

The exact size and make-up of committees will also vary. With an audit committee, for example, the general rule is that the numbers are appropriate to the complexity of the business/organisation and the risks it faces. An FT 350 company should have at least three IDs on its audit committee, as should an NHS Foundation Trust Board, while for smaller companies, that requirement falls to two. University Councils must 'be a small, well-informed authoritative body' and 'be composed of a majority of independent members' (who may also be drawn from the outside of the governing body).[2] Some committees, such as the nomination committee, may invite company executives to attend and provide further relevant insights about the business. However, it is crucial to avoid any conflicts of interests. The committee needs to act independently.

Remuneration committee

> If you want to take on a tough job, it's the remuneration committee deciding upon the salaries of the chief executive and all the other directors. They'll start off by saying: *Of course, we are a top-quartile company, so we should be paying top-quartile rates.* You won't be the most popular guy in the room if you say: *But this company is bottom-quartile in terms of performance. The salaries should reflect that.*

They will then wheel in a remuneration specialist, who will present the committee with graphs of where the board members are in relation to the competitors, and so on. It'll be quite overwhelming, with the executives wanting to go in one direction and the advisors, who are supposed to advise, clearly pushing in the same direction. And it's quite courageous to stand there and say; 'No, you're not going to get a million and a half. You're only worth £800,000.' It's not a job anybody would want.

Sir Peter Thompson, Former ID, British & Commonwealth and Pilkington's

To be an effective member of a remuneration committee (also known as Remco) requires a thorough understanding of the organisation and the various forces that shape remuneration. This includes all aspects of its size, from base salary levels, to annual bonus criteria, and performance measures, to revenues and margins.

As any remuneration committee member will be aware, pay awards are always keenly watched by the outside world, particularly when an organisation is perceived to have performed below par. There are no legal requirements to cap the level of directors' pay, not even for a company quoted on the stock market, but we've all seen the furore that often follows what is believed to be an unduly high pay and bonus settlement. This is the cue for outrage all round, accusations of 'fat cats', 'noses in troughs' and all sorts of other less than flattering analogies. This can be hugely damaging and disruptive to any organisation's reputation. Indeed, it can be damaging to an entire sector if pay awards are seen to be getting out of hand. Right now, it is likely that the headlines will be more critical than ever if organisations ignore what is going on in the wider world.

As we saw earlier, the university sector has been in the spotlight in particular over recent years, with accusations that some governing bodies are failing to keep a cap on what is perceived to be out-of-control salary inflation. In Chapter 4, I highlighted the controversial case of University of Bath vice chancellor Professor Dame Glynis Breakwell, who had a package totalling more than £468,000. Hers was an extreme example, but it is by no means isolated. Despite widespread calls for pay restraint from politicians, students and academics, universities are still sometimes giving vice chancellors what tabloid papers would call 'inflation-busting' pay awards. All this plays against a backdrop of plans to make staff cuts to stave off multi-million-pound budget deficits. One would have hoped that the remuneration committees of University Councils would have risen to the challenge.

The two key priorities of remuneration committees are clear cut: Determine the overall policies on executive compensation, and review compensation arrangements on a regular basis. This makes it all sound relatively straightforward, but this is not always the case. There are challenges all the way, and not just because an overbearing chief executive might feel entitled to greater rewards and recognition. There may be questions over whether it is prudent to pursue UK pay norms, or whether different measures need to be adopted for overseas directors who might compare their package to their competitors in the particular region. Likewise, there may be discussions around the size of rewards for directors in key roles such as technology, where there is often not enough talent to go around. Here, greater awards might be needed to retain important team members. Meanwhile, executive compensation needs to be fair and transparent.

The chair of the remuneration committee reports to the chairperson, working closely with him or her, as well as the CEO and HR director. As you can imagine, it can be a difficult balancing act to please everyone and will involve making some tough decisions that might not always be greeted positively by the executive team.

Audit committee

The audit committee takes care of the oversight of the integrity of an organisation's financial affairs, focusing on everything from the effectiveness of its internal control systems to the fair presentation of information in the financial statements. One of its key tasks is the appointment of an external auditor and to approve the terms of engagement with those auditors to ensure the quality of financial statements. It is wholly unsuitable that any executive team member is given free rein to shoehorn their favourite auditors into the process, for very obvious reasons.

In addition to the role of appointing and liaising with external auditors, audit committees are also specifically responsible for the checks and balances on the financial reporting process. Members check financial statements and clear any formal announcements about an organisation's financial performance. They will also take charge of reviewing internal financial controls and internal control and risk management systems. Everything is then reported back to the main board, with recommendations concerning where action or improvement is needed.

While external auditors are the professionals with the depth of financial expertise required, it is also important that the members of the audit committee are confident with a balance sheet. The penalties are high when this doesn't happen. When the full details of the Enron scandal unfolded in late 2001, the charge laid at the door of its audit committee was that its members simply didn't understand the complexities of the data being presented to them. This issue allowed the energy and services corporation to keep huge debts off its balance sheet with the aid of its auditor, Arthur Anderson, which was also alleged to have disguised excessive executive remuneration and manipulated the fudged accounts by presenting them in such a complex fashion. The ensuing scandal led to the bankruptcy and collapse of an organisation which was once named 'America's most innovative company' and employed 29,000 staff. In 2014, it was time for the audit committee of UK grocery giant Tesco to take its turn in the spotlight, after overstated profits of £263 million were revealed. While Tesco's then auditor PwC (which subsequently lost the business after 32 years in post) had raised concerns about Tesco's recording of commercial income, it took an internal whistle-blower to alert the board to the sheer scale of the problem. Tesco was fined £129 million over the affair and agreed with the

Financial Conduct Authority (FCA) to spend £85 million on compensating investors. These audit committee failures are not unique to the corporate world. In 2015, there was a financial scandal at the UK's largest mental health trust, which saw several clinical projects subsequently scrapped as a result. The West London Mental Health NHS Trust, a department responsible for funding large-scale capital projects, oversaw a £4 million overspend on unfunded or unapproved schemes. The trust, with an annual budget of £235 million, which runs 35 sites, had to call in anti-fraud specialists following allegations that financial documents had been altered to cover up mistakes.[3]

Anyone serving on an audit committee is required to keep up-to-date with any professional or regulatory requirements pertinent to the specific sphere of operations of the organisation. The audit committee may also cover whistleblowing policies and procedures. The committee chair plays an important role in ensuring the committee is allowed to perform its role freely and effectively.

All committees require relevant knowledge and skills, but the audit committee is perhaps the most technical and challenging. It is, after all, responsible for the financial health of an organisation and, in some cases, its very survival.

Nominations committee

The nominations committee is, as the name suggests, responsible for leading the board appointment process, recruiting both executive and IDs. Historically, this committee may sometimes have been a been a bit of a poor relation compared to audit and remuneration, but its importance is gaining traction as the benefits of diversity on boards is finally getting some much-deserved recognition.

Nominations committees now have an obligation to ensure all appointments are based on merit and objective criteria. Recruitment decisions should promote diversity of gender, social and ethnic backgrounds, cognitive and personal strengths. While initially concerned with board-level appointees, attention is now being turned to the executive pipeline to ensure diversity is a key consideration. Each sector has its own targets when it comes to diversity. Many campaigns, such as the Women in Sport, Beyond 30 campaign, have already been mentioned in this book. There is also an EU Non-Financial Reporting Directive that requires disclosures about diversity. It is inevitable that, even with Brexit, this will also remain on the agenda in the future since there are increasing calls for transparency about a board's actions and decisions.

It is the duty of boards to consider what composition is most likely to help it achieve its overall strategic aims. This may vary from organisation to organisation, or even over time. Ultimately, the three priorities of the nominations committee are to develop the talent pipeline, broaden the search for future directors and to look at the long-term strategy and resource accordingly.

Other committees

The existence and make-up of other committees will very much depend on the sector an organisation operates in. Any institution working in a high-risk environment will require a health and safety committee. This was certainly the case with Keller, the world's largest ground engineering firm, which I joined as an ID in 2001. Construction can be a dangerous business and midway through my term there, Keller suffered from a run of accidents which included several fatalities. When Roy Franklin took over as chairman in 2009, he pressed the board to make health and safety a priority. He had a background in the oil industry, where this is also a big issue, and saw the need for a number of improvements to be quickly identified and acted upon.

Quality committees are often found on NHS Trust boards and are responsible for providing assurance on all aspects of quality, such as delivery, governance, clinical risk management, workforce and information governance, research and development, and the regulatory standards of safety.

IDs are often expected to chair at least one board committee, which means expertise is required in the committee's area of focus.

In addition to the formal committees outlined here, there may be a requirement to sit on temporary working groups to scrutinise specific activities which are not necessarily a permanent feature of the organisation's main activities.

External consultants

According to the UK Corporate Governance Code 2018, IDs have a crucial role to play in the selection, appointment, reappointment and removal of external auditors to the audit committee of a quoted company and in approving their remuneration and terms of engagement. IDs are also in charge of reviewing and monitoring the external auditor's independence and, without a doubt, the external auditor should always report to the independent chair of the audit committee. Arguably, this rule should extend to all organisations and all committees where external consultants are engaged. Take, as an example, a remuneration committee. If a chief executive is allowed to take too much control over the process, it is inevitable that executive pay awards will not be given the rigorous scrutiny they deserve. The fact that a chief executive of a large-ish company can now make 140 times what the average person earns, whereas that figure used to be 40 times, shows how much this process has been abused in the past. The only way to rein it in is to put the decision completely into the hands of IDs, and that includes them liaising with any external consultants. It's a similar situation with the search committee. If we want to stamp out the situation where the CEO or other senior executives bring in people they know, flout the accepted practice and ignore calls for more diversity, IDs need to take control. They need to be the point of liaison with search consultants. Likewise, if an organisation appoints external financial advisors in the event of a takeover bid, the process should be entirely independent from the executives, who will have clear vested interests.

IDs need to have the strength, determination and courage to insist that they take control of any process that involves external consultants.

Board evaluation

Board evaluation has, for too long, been a highly informal process in far too many organisations. Indeed, recent evidence shows that only 20% of board evaluations are effective, according to a London Business School survey. It can be as simple as the chairman taking all the board members aside, one by one, and asking them how they thought it was all going. If everyone nods and says 'OK', then apparently nothing needs to be done. Indeed, even if misgivings are raised, there is little evidence that the process goes any further than a few reassurances that all would be alright shortly. After all, with no formal process in train, there's little impetus to follow through and make any real changes. Hardly surprisingly, after a wealth of scandals, board evaluation has been pinpointed as an area that needs to be changed. It has been widely agreed that boards need to actively scrutinise themselves and actively make changes where required.

In the UK, it is now a legal requirement for public companies to hold a board evaluation exercise every three years, although in my view this does not go far enough. It should be an annual event. While not a legal requirement in other sectors, it is certainly best practice to formalise this process. It should not be a box-ticking exercise either. The process should delve deeply into the culture, experience and behaviours necessary for the board to perform at its best. To make the process transparent, the results of the evaluation should be shared with key stakeholders and published in the annual report. Ideally, to answer the requirement to constantly improve board performance, organisations should be required to publish detailed board improvement plans. If applicable, this should certainly include a commitment to improve board diversity and more training for board members.

Formal board evaluation can be carried out externally, either by specialised consultants, or headhunting firms. For a full board evaluation checklist, please see Appendix B.

The actual process may vary a little, but it will centre around one-to-one interviews with individual board members. The information derived from these interviews is then compiled and presented in an anonymous report, which is presented to the chairman and the board. Experienced consultants may also make recommendations of possible improvements, based on examples of best practice seen elsewhere. They may advise on a new way to think about strategy, or suggest different approaches to tackling management succession.

The process will only be effective if steps are taken to correct any weaknesses that get identified through the evaluation. Failure to do so would render the entire exercise a waste of time and money.

It should be said that a formal process should not mean that the more informal 'How is everything going?' chats should be stopped altogether. They should not – in fact, they are extremely valuable when it comes to keeping a watchful eye on any board and the dynamics that drive it. I would advise any chairman to regularly have one-to-ones with individual board members to gauge the temperature of the boardroom.

Ultimately, boards are powerful institutions and there are plenty of examples throughout this book of what happens when they don't function as they should. It is beholden on any organisation to take whatever steps possible to ensure its senior team can work together constructively. IDs have a huge role to play in this endeavour.

Notes

1 https://www.mckinsey.com/business-functions/strategy-and-corporate-finance/our-insights/improving-board-governance-mckinsey-global-survey-results, August 2013.
2 The Higher Education Code of Governance, December 2014.
3 https://www.independent.co.uk/life-style/health-and-families/health-news/broadmoor-financial-scandal-the-4m-of-nhs-funds-wasted-at-high-security-hospital-a6760496.html

Chapter 7
Finding the right independent director position

There are three Golden Rules for people to follow if they are serious about becoming an independent director:

Rule 1 – First, determine what your unique set of skills are, why you are different and stand out from the crowd and why you should be hired. A CV doesn't cover this since it just states what you have done. What's important is the thinking behind it, as well as what your career has given you and why you did the things you did. Realistically, you should be able to articulate this in less than two minutes.

Rule 2 – Adopt a rifle shot approach, not a shotgun! Be very clear about what you want to do and intend to do. Don't present yourself as unsure, undecided, or that you could do this or that. Be bold. Leave the impression that you know what you are going to do and if a contact can't help you, then perhaps they would be kind enough to refer you to someone who can. A strong articulation of intent will be remembered. This is really important for network referrals.

Rule 3 – Network, network, network! This is critical. Talk to ALL your contacts and push the boundaries. Keep the network going. It needs to be worked at constantly. The importance of this can't be understated. It is time-consuming and hard work, but it always pays off if you apply Rules 1 and 2.

Alan McWalter, Portfolio Chairman/ID Including Chair Newmarket Travel

Before you leap in and start applying for an ID position, it is well worth pausing for a moment and carefully planning your ID strategy. Much thought needs to be given to the type of role/organisation that would best suit your mix of skills and the experience you are hoping to gain from your involvement.

Something we haven't discussed until now is the possibility of taking up several ID positions as part of what is known as a plural career. Here, after a period of reflection, an individual may have decided that they no longer want one single day job, but would prefer to spread their interests across a range of organisations, serving on a range of boards. In this case, this is the time to consider the make-up of the ideal portfolio for your own set of skills and interests. A good mix might be, say, one public company board, one substantial private company, one start-up and one charity, or University Council. In this case, it would be prudent to secure the public company ID position first as an 'anchor' position, and then slot the other ID roles around it. The reason for doing it in this order is down to the way that public company boards, indeed public companies, are run, according to strict rules and regulations. The time commitments of an ID will therefore usually be very well-defined, with meetings often planned well in advance. In contrast, private companies, or volunteer roles, might be less organised or predictable, and meeting dates may be frequently moved. All of this does, of course, need to be weighed up against the fact that board positions on large, quoted companies are not easy to come by. There are a finite number of vacant positions and a lot of eminently well-qualified candidates chasing them. In contrast, board roles with charitable trusts and sporting

https://doi.org/10.1515/9783110706123-007

bodies are easier to come by, as they get considerably fewer applications, although that may now change in the new, more community-aware, environment. University Councils tend to be fairly well subscribed, perhaps because there is a certain amount of prestige about being associated with one of the country's key intellectual establishments.

> After 26 years in positions of operational and strategic responsibility within the pharmaceutical sector, at C-suite and board level, I had a decision to make. Do I go into another full-time job, or do I do something different? Another full-time job would have meant doing something very similar to what I had been doing. I also wanted to travel less and have a bit more time to pursue other interests.
>
> Once I decided on a plural career, I wanted to build my portfolio slowly. I liked the idea of settling myself into each role before looking for the next one.
>
> **Dipti Amin, Independent Director, Cambridge Innovation Capital, University of Hertfordshire, Buckinghamshire Healthcare Trust**

At this initial stage, it is also important to consider very carefully the size of board that you sign up to. According to a study by researchers at Texas A&M University,[1] the size and complexity of a board, including the number of directors and their outside obligations, can be a barrier to it functioning effectively. If a board is too large and unwieldy, there could well be structural reasons why it is almost impossible to do the job well. To have an impact and prevent any prospect of an ID role spiralling into disaster, it might be prudent to look at positions on smaller boards where possible, certainly when it comes to the first role. If you have an eye on a future plural career, it's quite helpful to cut your teeth with voluntary positions on charities and social enterprises, which tend to have leaner boards than established corporates.

Although there is a recognised need for a more diverse, skilled pool of talent, securing that first ID role requires as much perseverance, planning and tenacity as acquiring any executive role. Since ID roles are business critical, whatever sector you gravitate to, boards will naturally lean towards people with prior experience. While previous work within similar organisations is good, previous executive or ID roles will often trump it. In fact, searching for an appropriate position is not unlike going back to square one of your career. You know, the catch-22 scenario where you can't get your first job without experience, but you can't get experience if you don't have a first job.

Begin your strategy by working out how to get noticed by the type of organisations you'd like to join and how to raise your profile generally so that when something does come up, your name has a chance of getting on the list. The perfect start-point here is to do what you'd do when beginning any job hunt: organise your CV. A well-written CV can really improve your chances, just as a CV does in any other competitive environment for senior positions. As we all know, quite often, CVs are given barely a few seconds of attention before they are either placed in the 'must-see' or reject pile. It is therefore essential to know how you can improve your outlook with the perfect ID CV.

Writing the model ID CV

When planning a CV, it helps to think about it as a marketing exercise for yourself. It needs to be a factual presentation of your most relevant experience and skills, together with an indication of your potential, but written in the most compelling, readable way. Ideally, you'll be looking at just two pages, but this is not an excuse to squash the font-size down to 8 points so you can include everything you have ever done since leaving school. Be selective! Besides, if your CV looks difficult to read, or too turgid, it could immediately end up in the slush pile.

Focus your attention on writing a powerful opening. Rather like a good book: If you haven't grabbed the reader and drawn them in within the first few lines, you may have lost their attention forever. Thus, after the essential basics (name, address and contact details), begin with a two or three line 'networking message'. Think of it in terms of your own mini elevator pitch advertising your skills, and include what you are doing now and what you want to achieve. If you have previously identified a requirement for a specific skill, or subject matter expertise, include it. It's a great way to make a quick impact. Avoid cliché, waffle, soft skills, or excessive detail: brevity is best. Likewise, don't slip into jargon or try to impress by using long words. What is it that sums you up in the most efficient, compelling way? Some examples might include:

– For an executive with no previous ID experience, looking for a role as a trustee on an internationally focused charity:

Successful PLC COO in the international logistics sector now pursuing a portfolio career focused on independent director roles. Deep expertise in road and air freight operations. Looking to become a trustee for a charity where international operations are a key component of future growth.

– Alternatively, for an experienced executive looking for an ID role in the education sector, to run alongside their executive role:

HR Director at a FTSE 250 PLC in technology with permission from my employer to undertake an external independent director (ID) appointment. Deep expertise in company transformation and growth strategy, with an excellent understanding of the ID role. Looking to join a university council where my experience and perspectives will contribute to a high-performing board.

– Targeting a role on an NHS Trust board:

Experienced project director and consultant, specialising in the turnaround of merged PCTs, rationalisation plans for hospital sites and the preparation of Foundation Trust applications, now pursuing an appointment to an NHS Trust. Deep expertise in secured turnarounds of organisations under threat due to financial position and management restructuring.

Note that, in each case, the applicant has put their existing job title upfront. It's a quick way to establish credibility and experience. Also, if the applicant has held a non-executive role, or executive role in the past, in the relevant industry, this is the time to establish it upfront.

It can be difficult writing an interesting, pithy and compelling networking message. Don't fall into the trap of staring at a blank page in a blind panic, though. The best advice is to get something down and then work at refining it. When you think you are nearly there, leave it for 24 hours and then come back to it. It's the equivalent of looking at it with fresh eyes and you'll be able to give it a final tweak to really tighten it up.

Follow-up the networking message with a profile section. This is another crucial part of the 'attention grabbing' stage. It's what people review before scrolling down on their computer, laptop, or even mobile and you don't want anyone switching to the next email in the list before they've given your application full scrutiny. It will include three or four short paragraphs expanding on the networking message, with each paragraph focusing on a different point that sums you up in the most efficient way. Key areas to cover are pertinent details of your background, current career, what you are looking for and why you are the best choice for any role.

The same rules apply here as for the networking message: make each word count. Use short sentences, common language and avoid excessive detail.

Next, move on to describe any previous executive board experience, if applicable. You might want to set it out in a neat table, but beware of becoming too fancy with the layout. You are not selling your services as an IT technician. Bright colours, ALL CAPITALS, and any font other than Arial, Times New Roman or Calibri is not recommended.

If you have already got an ID position, or have previously held one, the next section should list them. Break it down into current and previous ones and, again, it might work well to present them in a neat, well-spaced, table.

Don't assume the reader will automatically be familiar with the companies you've worked for, or the actual role that you did. Include some (brief) detail, explaining what the company does and your responsibilities there. Highlight any achievements that were a direct result of your efforts. Likewise, think in terms of key words that answer the ID brief, such as specific skillsets, a cooperative, collaborative approach, or examples of advisory-related achievements. The aim is to demonstrate a broad range of experience in different capacities, different industries or different geographies. It really helps to have skills that no one else on the board currently has.

After this, the following sections should showcase in order: your senior executive career, executive career, professional qualifications and education, and any language skills. End with the web link to your LinkedIn profile, which will, of course, be completely up to date. Ensure too that it matches your CV, something that sometimes gets forgotten when you update one, but neglect to alter the other.

Networking

That old adage 'It's not what you know, but who you know' is as true here as it is anywhere else. While management search agencies and head-hunters are the traditional go-to paths to finding out about, and applying for, a great many ID roles, don't miss out on this vital first step.

Ask yourself: Who do I know who can help me? When any board is considering making an appointment, a similar question will be asked: Who do we know? Likewise, head-hunters and consultants will ask the same thing when given the search brief for a new ID appointment. An absolute priority for any aspiring ID is to let all their contacts know that they are in the market for this type of position. Human nature dictates that people prefer to appoint someone they know, or at least know something about because someone else has told them about a particular person. It is your task to make that person you.

Your strategy will be the polar opposite of when you have sought to change executive roles in the past. Here, discretion is key. The last thing you want is for your senior managers, or close colleagues to hear that you are considering jumping ship. Likewise, it can make things awkward with key customers or supply contacts. When you are seeking an ID position though, the more you shout about it, the better. Maximise the power of your personal network.

At the simplest level, if you want to join a local organisation, get down there and speak to them. Get to know the people involved and make it clear you have something to offer. This is not a one-off activity. Make sure you are a regular and take an active interest.

If you are looking further afield, you will need to cast the net wider. Most people have built up hundreds, possibly thousands of contacts over the years. Anyone with any sort of experience in senior roles will most likely have a long list of LinkedIn connections, plus at least 1,000 business contacts' numbers in their phone. With this broad use of contacts, you'll have 100 or so *key relationships*. These are people you have previously worked closely with, either directly as colleagues or in some sort of supply/customer relationship. Invariably, you will have got on well and the work was a success. These people will remain predisposed to helping you, where they can, for a long time. Your plan A is to identify these people and let them know about your ID aspirations. Pick up the phone or send them an email and tell them that you have ambitions to secure an ID role. Be specific about where you believe your skills lie, particularly in terms of that all-important functional expertise. You will be amazed how many people will respond to this sort of focussed approach. Even if it doesn't lead to an immediate opening, which it very rarely does (although it can and does happen), it will open a lot of doors. Your contacts will keep their eyes and ears open for you and when they do hear of something, however vague, your name will come to mind simply because you have taken the time to inform them of your ID plans. This might lead to referral or an introduction to someone else, or possibly talks about a specific role, and off you go.

If all of your 100 key contacts make just two suggestions, that is 200 pieces of new information, whether it is a person, a company, an idea or a recalibration of your elevator pitch. If that cycle is repeated, that in turn leads to 400 new ideas. Within two steps, you have gone from 100 contacts to 600 suggestions. Of course, there will duplication, non-responders and people who genuinely can't help, but the point here is that simply asking people for a couple of suggestions can be very powerful.

> As soon as the idea of a securing an ID role comes onto an executive's radar, they should start thinking about where they want to go and then preparing for it. Looking for board experience within your own organisation is a good place to start. Large companies can be difficult places to secure a directorship, even for very senior executives. However, these types of organisations often set up special purpose vehicles to oversee joint ventures, or to hold specific assets, or to silo investments made elsewhere. These entities will require properly constituted boards for governance and oversight purposes which means directorships akin to 'internal ID' appointments may be available. Try to secure one of these positions, because landing the first external ID role, especially as part of a portfolio career, is the hardest piece of the jigsaw and previous board experience carries value and weight. You may have to explore different internal networks than your current department and contacts. In addition to asking your boss and the HR department, the in-house legal team and/or company secretary are two good lines of enquiry.
>
> **Mike Clancy, Founder, NED Career Services, Walgrove**

Working with critical relationships does take effort and strategy. These contacts are invariably busy people with their own careers. It is not simply a case of mentioning your ID ambitions once and hoping they'll come back to you at some point. You might need to engineer three or four nudges along the way to remind them that you're in the market. If it is done skilfully, tactfully and respectfully, they won't mind at all.

The point to bear in mind here is: This is networking. It's just the same thing as you have always done in your business career. The only difference is, in the past, you've done it for your employer and now you are doing it for yourself. In all cases, networking is a reciprocal activity. If you go in with a 'me, me, me' attitude, you may very well ruin some good, long-term contacts. Be sure to build on your previous solid relationship before making any specific requests. This will entail making networking part of your day-to-day activities, rather than a one-off event, clumsily designed for the 'big ask'. When you do speak about your ambitions, be specific. That networking message you opened your CV with will come in handy here. It is a succinct summary of what you want to do and what you feel you can offer. Practice it, so it sounds natural when you say it, rather than repeating it by rote. Most of all, be patient. Networking rarely produces instant results. You need to be resilient and prepared to play the long game.

The best advice I received was: Don't undervalue your existing relationships – they will create opportunities. For six months after my KPMG retirement date, I talked to my key connections, and outlined my plans and ambitions. Two eggs hatched from those discussions, and I am almost four years into those hugely enjoyable NED roles.

Jonathan Hurst, Portfolio NED including NED at Addleshaw Goddard Solicitors

The formal application routes

Plan B, which will run alongside Plan A, is to cast the net wider. The approach will vary, depending upon the position you are seeking. I have broken down the potential avenues to pursue in the following sections.

Corporate – public and private companies

It is rare to see ID positions advertised for listed or private companies. If the posts are advertised, you are most likely to find them in *The Financial Times*, *The Times* and *The Guardian*. Public companies in particular will generally give their ID brief to head-hunters or search firms, many of which specialise in recruiting for ID roles. This is, in part, to demonstrate that they are pursuing a vigorous, objective, fair and transparent process. Anyone interested in this sort of appointment should seek to develop relationships with a number of search firms, all of which can be found with a simple online search. Sources you might like to look at can be found in Appendix C.

The onus is always on a search firm to ask you to consider joining an organisation, rather than an aspiring ID applying to do so. It therefore stands to reason that you should make yourself as visible as possible with a wide range of recruiters. Fortunately, search firms are always keen to hear about talented people who might not yet be on their radar. They will often agree to a getting-to-know-you interview to increase their pool of potential IDs.

It is useful to understand the process of working with a search firm, which can take up to four months. Generally, it goes like this:

- The client starts the ball rolling by calling in a search consultant and outlining the brief.
- The search consultant will then be given access to other directors to gain a better understanding of board culture and style, so they can work out what sort of individual would be most effective in that setting.
- A structured research exercise follows, which results in a long list of around 12 to 15 names.
- Individual candidates are contacted and interviewed by the search firm.

- Detailed, written presentations about each relevant candidate are sent to the client.
- The client will shortlist three or four candidates, who will each be invited in for interview.
- An offer is made, references are taken and a contract is signed.

There are a number of other avenues to explore in addition to search firms. Advisory firms such as accountancy and law firms and management consultancies should certainly be on your target list. Many run specific networking events for IDs.

In addition, there are a number of networking organisations set up for the exact purpose of assisting people into their first ID role. Many of them are fee-based networking groups, which might also offer training courses to help aspiring IDs with specific skills. *Women on Boards* is a free service, although subscribed members are offered a broad range of benefits. This organisation has proved to be an important pipeline in helping women and boasts that it supports five board successes a week, both the supply and demand side. As well as advising and assisting candidates, it also liaises with companies that are recruiting. ID positions are advertised through its NED Vacancy Board.

Another handy and free resource is KPMG's *Connect on Board*. It was set up with the aim to attract more people from diverse backgrounds and assist them in finding an appropriate ID role. To join, you will need to submit a CV showing a solid foundation of executive roles and details of any previous board experience. There is also a requirement for a thorough awareness of corporate governance issues and of the business sector as a whole. Candidates are all subject to a verification process. Organisations looking to fill ID positions are also required to register before advertising new roles.

> When I began actively looking for new ID roles, I contacted all the head-hunters. I made sure people knew all about me. I am also a member of *Criticaleye*, initially as an executive member, then as a corporate member. It proved really useful. They organise different events and round tables, which have the twin benefits of providing knowledge and a practical perspective. It's a great way to improve your network and get involved in discussions about current issues. They also bring in experts, so you can tap them for advice. I also speak at events, which is a great way to improve your visibility and understand more about any opportunities.
> **Devyani Vaishampayan, Managing Partner, HR TECH Partnership**

In every case, whichever organisations you sign up with, resolve to be an active (and noticeable) member of the group. As well as regularly attending and participating in events, find out about opportunities for taking speaking engagements and writing articles/blogs for publication in their marketing output.

Public sector

For roles with the NHS, as well as with regulatory bodies, museums and advisory bodies, you should register with the *Centre for Public Appointments*. Candidates specify what they are interested in and receive email notifications when new appointments are published that match specifications. The improvement.nhs.uk website also publishes all details of NHS provider vacancies and maintains a 'talent database' of board-ready people across the UK. It is open to receiving details of potential candidates.

Not all NHS appointments happen in this way. Dipti Amin, who began her ID portfolio as a non-executive director on the Board of the Buckinghamshire Healthcare NHS Trust, took a different route. Dipti, who had a career in senior posts in the pharmaceutical industry, after gaining her medical degree from Guys and St Thomas' Medical Schools of the University of London, was keen to move her career to the next stage with a portfolio of ID positions. Her starting point was NHS Trusts and she contacted a recruitment firm about an advertised position but it had just closed for application. They subsequently contacted her when another post came up, this time with the Buckinghamshire Healthcare NHS Trust. The post particularly intrigued Dipti, since the Trust had recently had issues raised by a Care Quality Commission inspection and were actively taking measures to improve things – she liked the challenge that presented.

'It sounded like a good opportunity,' she said. 'I wanted to be somewhere where I could use my experience to help make something happen.'

Charity

Charity boards are solely made up of independent trustees – in other words, there are no executive directors. Trustee positions are increasingly being advertised online via social media and, in particular, on Twitter and LinkedIn, with groups like *Young Charity Trustees*. Draw up a list of organisations that interest you, perhaps because you have experience in the particular field or the charity is relevant to your local community, then follow all of the organisations on your list and actively participate by responding to their posts. Charities appreciate it when people are proactive and supportive.

The Charities Commission also runs an annual Trustees' Week, which aims to showcase more about what trustees do and highlight opportunities. Events are free and held across the UK. For smaller charities, there is a handy trustee-finder website, *do-it.org*, which is a partnership between Small Charities Coalition and Do It.

There is an onus on charities to make it feel like an impactful role, when they are trying to recruit people. They know that if they position it as 'This is just something on the side' or 'You've very generous in helping us', people won't value the position. They need to be seen to be offering fulfilling roles. By the same token, though, they are not just ready to accept anyone that shows an interest. They are on the lookout for people who want to make a real difference. They can spot someone a mile off who is just looking to add a bit of colour to their CV, or whose boss has told them that it might be good to have a charity appointment as part of their development plan. Charities are serious businesses and need to be taken seriously.

Patrick Dunne, ID Roles Include Boardelta, EY Foundation, ESSA and Leap

Sport

For positions on organisations in sport, uksport.gov.uk is a good place to start. The resource advertises board vacancies by type of support and region. The *Sport and Recreation Alliance* – the umbrella organisation for the governing bodies of 320 members, from the FA, to the Rugby Football Union, to UK Athletics, to British Rowing and the Exercise, Movement and Dance Partnership – is another useful gateway for anyone seeking an ID in sport. Its Alliance Directors club offers members courses to hone their skills, build up professional networks and insight into ID roles in sport and recreation.

There is, of course, no substitute for starting from 'the inside' and already being familiar with the sport in question. Olympic gold medal winning Paralympian Liz Johnson started her career serving on sporting boards while she was still competing. Liz, who was selected for Team GB at the age of just 14 years old and who went on to win gold at 100m breaststroke at the Paralympics in Beijing, was the British Swimming Board's athletes' representative for the Paralympic squad for six years. It was her first experience of sitting on a board and she really enjoyed it from the start.

'I realised that I was in a position to help others on the team,' she said. 'I could make changes and make things better for them. As an athlete myself, I could see how the decisions that were being made at the boardroom table were having an impact back in the pool.'

After retiring from the sport, Liz was invited to join the board of Disability Sport Wales. One of her responsibilities there has been to set up a separate 'youth board' that represents, mentors and empowers young disabled athletes.

'These young people need mentoring because they obviously haven't sat on a board before, but it is the right thing to do because they are so much closer to the demographic that uses the service.

'There are a lot of people who are passionate about a particular sport, who are more than capable of being brilliant board members, but they don't know how to get involved. If they do see an advert, they don't think that advert is meant for them. You don't need to be important to serve on a board. You just need to want to make a difference.'

Universities, further education colleges and schools

At present, 50% of University Council[2] positions are made without public advertisement. Candidates are approached directly, after being identified by other board members as potentially suitable. Vacancies that are advertised tend to appear in the higher education recruitment sections of *The Times* or *The Guardian*. Anyone interested in school governorships can register and apply via www.governorsfor schools.org.uk. The website also has a lot of useful facts and background on school governor positions.

My colleague Richard Atkins – who serves alongside me on the University of Exeter Council, as well as being the Further Education Commissioner for England, with responsibility for leading on quality improvements in further education and Sixth Form Colleges – has firm views on how educational establishments can up their game when it comes to recruiting IDs.

'University boards need to be active and have dedicated search committees,' Richard says. 'There is no point siting there, waiting for the right person to come along, or identifying a friend of a friend. I don't think advertising is particularly effective, either.'

His view is that strong University Councils have made a point of identifying the skill sets they require and then have actively approached individuals or organisations with the right abilities. Thus, if there was a need for a highly numerate person to fill a position on the audit committee, then he'd advocate approaching the Chartered Institute of Accountants to ask for recommendations.

'Ideally, they will identify one or two people who might be suitable, and then it is a university's job to invite them in and persuade them,' Richard continued. 'We live in a very busy world, and some people will say no. However, universities need to convince suitable candidates that there is a lot more to it, over and above being altruistic. Serving on a University Council is a great thing to have on your CV if you are still in the world of employment. If you are out of that, it is a good way to remain engaged and keep the brain ticking over.'

What if a university is in trouble? As we have already seen, many universities are in a particularly vulnerable position. Would that make the job of University Councils even harder when it comes to persuading suitable recruits?

Not so, says Richard Atkins. Through his role as Further Education Commissioner, Richard has been involved with issues at Hadlow College in Kent. The institution became the first in the country to go into educational administration in May 2019, thanks to 'inadequate financial health'. Governance has been identified as the root of the problem.

'We've identified skills that will be needed to improve an organisation that has not been doing well at all. Obviously, there is a requirement for educational experience, but there is a definite need for financial expertise too. We'd also need property experience, since there is a lot of property involved.'

'Interestingly, when you sit down with the right individuals and try to persuade them, they are generally fairly keen. Many people would often rather join a failing organisation than a successful one. They enjoy the challenge of turnaround more than sitting on top of something that is already very successful indeed.'

Informal routes

Not all of the organisations that are looking for IDs to join will have formal application processes. This is certainly the case with smaller community groups, sports clubs and volunteer organisations. In this case, the easiest way to put your hat in the ring as a potential committee member is when you already have some sort of association with the group. You will have shown a clear interest, possibly regularly attending meetings and will know the key people involved. Explain that you are keen to do more, and it is very likely they will welcome your participation with open arms.

If you are keen to volunteer, but don't yet have a firm view on what to do or where, take your time. Visit your community's library, read local news sources and speak to people you know who live nearby. Anyone with a full-time job should find out if their employer is already running an ESV scheme. They may well already have links with certain organisations and, if they do, this will dovetail nicely with what you are trying to do. If you put yourself forward to volunteer, the processes will already be in place to pave the way for the link. Alternatively, you could look at a number of organisations to help source volunteers, such as Business in the Community, via the Prince's Responsible Business Network: bitc. org.uk.

Training

To close this chapter, I would like to touch upon the question of training for an ID role. The benefits of promoting and achieving professional standards in a variety of careers have been recognised for decades, if not centuries. Yet, the fact that there is no legal requirement for training in order to become an ID has always been a surprise to many. After all, you need training for almost every other important senior position. Accountants need qualifications, engineers need qualifications and dentists, doctors and teachers need qualifications. On a more personal level, if you want to drive a car alone on the highway, you need to have passed a test. Yet when it comes to taking one of the most important roles in any organisation, where you are its long-term custodian and personally liable if things go wrong, there is no compulsory qualification. There is a great quote, ascribed to many different authors, from Derek Bok, to Ann Landers, which sums this up down to a tee in my view: *If you think training is expensive, try ignorance.* While there have been a number of representations made to correct this glaring error, some of which have been made by myself, to date there is no sign of any action being taken.

Compulsory or otherwise, there are no circumstances where I wouldn't recommend spending some additional preparation time taking one of the many courses on offer which will give you a grounding in the knowledge and skills required. There are many courses available, and the length and intensity of the one you choose should be commensurate with the type of ID position you are hoping to get. If you wanted to take up a position as a school governor, you would require guidance that is completely different from someone who is targeting a FTSE 100 boardroom slot. However, there is a strong argument that anyone considering a school governor role would be wise to devote some time to learning at least the basics, such as how to read a balance sheet. Educational establishments are increasingly run like small businesses. Likewise, charities, sporting bodies and, of course, the NHS, are all dealing with huge quantities of money. Either way, there are many training options available which will equip you with the knowledge of what you will be expected to do and the range of your responsibilities. The courses will also give you a full rundown of your liabilities and obligations – in fact, everything you need to hit the ground running from day one.

A selection of courses worth consideration is listed in Appendix D.

There will, of course, be gaps in what you can learn, since many ID courses are run over just one or two days. There is, for example, often very little time spent on communication and social media and on how an ID should deal with it, even though it is an increasingly important part of any position. If you are considering a portfolio ID career, you might like to consider further studies in this direction and also courses that are specific to the sectors you choose.

Another option that any first time ID might consider is a boardroom apprenticeship. This is very much along the lines of a traditional apprenticeship. However, while plumbers may spend up to four years learning the ropes with their mentors, boardroom apprentices can do it in 12 months. The not-for-profit organisation Board Apprentice,[3] which aims to increase the number and diversity of candidates for ID roles, runs the scheme which allows apprentices to shadow all the activities of board members. They get to do everything from attending sub-committee meetings, to the annual meeting, to board dinners. There are also workshops offered by Deloitte and mentoring sessions. It's a great way to avoid the catch-22 situation where people are excluded from board appointments because they have no boardroom experience.

Notes

1 Steven Boivie, Michael K. Bednar, Ruth V. Aguilera and Joel Andrus, Are Boards Designed to Fail? The Implausibility of Effective Board Monitoring, *The Academy of Management Annals*, Vol. 10, Issue 1, pp. 319–407, 28 January 2016.
2 Leadership Foundation survey.
3 https://www.boardapprentice.com

Chapter 8
Interviews, contracts and fees

When Devyani Vaishampayan began to weigh up her options for ID roles with UK firms, she was quick to reject any tick-box approach. She didn't want to be the token woman, or BAME, on the team. In fact, she never considered her role that way. While she had a very well-formulated strategy about what organisations to approach and how to attract their attention, that strategy was based around the demand for her very specific skill sets.

Devyani pinpointed that one of her key selling points was her international experience. As well as having a career working for large corporates, she had previously served as an ID on boards in India, Singapore and the UK, each with very different requirements. In India, Devyani was on the board of a private fund and was asked to head up the strategy for growth and to formalise the proposition. The role in Singapore was with one of the country's oldest charity organisations, which was a highly respected institution steeped in culture. There was a delicate line to walk between creating public trust while also raising as much awareness as possible about campaigns, while also respecting the very strict and traditional hierarchy at the board-level of this not-for-profit organisation. Her UK appointment is with the British Quality Foundation, a membership organisation that is highly reliant on membership sales and which is therefore very focused on financial viability.

In Devyani's view, the breadth of the roles meant she had developed a valuable, wide-ranging skillset through the experience, with many of these skills being in great demand elsewhere. If you understand the focus of the role, it is possible to add value.

'I know of many boards which are running a very international business, yet they have no one with true international experience,' Devyani says. 'There are so many changes going on in this environment, particularly with emerging markets, it just makes sense to have someone with experience who can shape the business agenda.'

'Specific skillsets are going to become much more important as time goes on. It's no longer a case of sticking with tick-box requirement for traditional backgrounds and purely functional expertise. We have gone far beyond IDs playing a pure governance role. The balance has to change and there are signs that it is.'

—

After all the work scrutinising adverts, preparing a CV, networking and getting to know search agencies, it may be tempting to jump into the first ID role you are offered. Or certainly, into the interview/shortlisting process. I would, however, advise very strongly against this. Or, as I am fond of saying, if you jump on the first bus, it may be going to Southend, whereas the one just behind it is heading off the

https://doi.org/10.1515/9783110706123-008

Caribbean. It's not that there is anything wrong with Southend, but you get my drift.

Whether you are looking for a mixed portfolio as part of a new plural career, or just one ID position to expand your horizons while still working in a full-time role elsewhere, the choice of the first role you take is crucial. Certainly, if something comes up and you are invited to apply, it is worth pausing for a moment to give it full consideration before you get too far involved in the recruitment process.

Key elements to weigh the potential role up against are:

Integrity

Do you believe you have the expertise, experience and skill sets required to do justice to the position being described? You should only ever allow your name to be put forward for positions where you believe you can be an effective member of the board. Reflection on this point is now more important than ever. Not only is your professional reputation at stake, but you are also taking on a role where you will have personal liabilities. There is limited opportunity to learn on the job. The penalties for getting it wrong are high.

Objectivity

For paid roles in the corporate sector or certain trusts, remind yourself that the financial reward can potentially reduce your objectivity. Ignore the remuneration if you want to make an informed, unbiased decision.

Research

Get a good feel for the technical and regulatory requirements which impact the organisation in question and which will, therefore, dictate your responsibilities as an ID. If you have not already been provided with one, request a detailed specification on the role. Check also if there is a comprehensive induction programme for new directors. (For more details on onboarding, see the next chapter.) If a head-hunter is involved in the process, they should be able to provide you with much of this information.

Consider, too, who else is on the board you are looking at. This may very well be a big factor in your decision-making, particularly if there is an opportunity to work with a good chair who you respect, or to gain exposure to experienced IDs from other industries.

The final consideration will, of course, be logistics. Aside from the time commitments, which are particularly pertinent if you already have a full-time role or indeed other ID positions, there is also the question of location. It takes time to travel to meetings, after all. If you are also allowing for potential committee involvement, this can substantially add to the pressure on your schedule.

Ultimately, you will have to exercise a degree of professional judgement on the decision whether or not to move forward. If it doesn't feel right or doesn't tick all the boxes, this is a good time to bow out gracefully and return to your search for a more suitable ID role. You may, however, feel that any concerns have been adequately addressed, or be very keen indeed on being considered. In this case, you will go forward to the interview stage.

An interview for any ID position is quite a bit different to one for any executive or senior role. The focus is not whether or not you can do a particular job. Interviewers need to be satisfied that you can add value at board level and that your views and values are in alignment with theirs. They'll be thinking about how you will fit into the existing team and whether or not you'll be a good balance between the roles of executives and IDs.

> One of the most important starting points is to think: Why would the board choose you? What is it about your core background, experiences and insight that you will be able to bring that will be particularly valuable?
>
> A helpful piece of advice that I was given before I got my first ID role was to write a personal marketing plan. Write down on one piece of paper why you are the person they are looking for. Be really clear and explicit about your strengths.
>
> **Ruth Cairnie, Chair Babcock International, Non-Executive Rolls Royce,**
> **Associated British Foods and ContourGlobal**

General notes on the interview process

As with any interview, preparation is key. If you are shortlisted for an interview, you need to do your homework to carefully research the organisation ahead of that dialogue. The 'So what do you know about us?' question is a bit of a classic, and it comes up nearly every time in one form or another. There is no excuse not to have a coherent answer. Dig back into an organisation's history, using both the company's own resources and a Google search of press stories. If there are any independent reports, read them. If applicable, review the advert for the role, so you know exactly what skills they want. Alternatively, if your name was put forward by a head-hunter or search agency, ask for some advance guidance on what the interviewer will be looking for. Pay particular attention to any recent developments or changes in direction in that organisation due to the pandemic. The question is broad enough to offer a good opportunity for you to steer the discussion towards your own areas of expertise or experience and how they'd be helpful to this specific organisation. Rehearse a few answers that meet this brief.

Likewise, you may like to prepare for a few of the other most commonly asked questions at interviews for ID roles. These include:

- Why do you want this role?
- What challenges have you faced in the past, and how have you dealt with them?

- Can you give examples of how you have influenced change, or challenged decisions in the past?
- What mistakes have you made, and how have you learned from them?

If you do not have prior ID experience, interviewers may probe to find out whether you fully understand the difference between being an executive and an ID. It is worth considering what experience you have had of working with IDs in the past. Have any helped you in a particular way or inspired you?

It is highly likely that you will be asked about specifics on your CV, just as you would in any other interview. If you have adjusted the CV you submitted to show how your skills and experience match up to the requirements of the organisation, now is the time to check through that CV again. Check for any gaps that you might need to explain, or details that would be useful to expand upon.

On the actual day itself, leave plenty of time to get to the interview location and don't forget to bring along any board information that you have been sent in advance.

The interview itself will most likely cover four key areas:

Personality questions
The questions can be quite informal and are designed to get a better feel for the interviewee's personality. Potential IDs need to be confident and articulate and able to show that they'd make an active contribution to the boardroom. Those who can demonstrate great people skills and who are comfortable challenging others will score well.

Don't, however, fall into the trap of feeling you need to be 'forthright' if that is not your usual style. Boardrooms are made up of many different personality types. It may be that this particular board is already fully stocked with outspoken individuals and is on the lookout for someone who is more thoughtful and considered in their approach. Either way, honesty is best. Be yourself.

Decision-making questions
These questions probe for a candidate's decision-making skills to see how they react to problems and challenges within the organisation. Again, it is not a case of one-size-fits-all. Not all boards are looking for someone who asks too many difficult questions. Certainly not the ones that have become too cosy and a little complacent. You will have to take the temperature of the room to see what sort of candidate they might prefer. Then you will need to take a view on whether or not you want to join a board where too much independent thought is frowned upon.

Leadership questions
IDs should be good leaders. This section of the interview explores how they might offer leadership in specific instances and demonstrate whether or not a candidate has the skills and ability to hold executives to account.

Strategic questions

This is where your prior research will come into its own, as the interviewer switches to more technical questions on the strategic development of the organisation. They will look to test your knowledge about the organisation and the sector it operates within. This is the time to show that you have researched and understood the board's strategic objectives, and the risks and challenges it currently faces, and that you can make a useful contribution in the future direction of the organisation.

There will also be practical questions to assess a candidate's commitment and the amount of days per year they can commit to travel and meetings. Some organisations need more input than others, depending upon their current status, and may need an ID who can offer more support and time. Expect to be asked about how you will balance the role with other commitments, whether it is a full-time job or other ID positions.

No two interviews are the same, and you need to be sensitive to different styles. While much has been made of the need of the growing requirement for specific skills, be wary of talking too much about your specialism, unless prompted. The board might conclude that you do not have a broad enough skill set to make a wider contribution.

Following the interview, there may be further stages where candidates are invited to meet other board members. If you progress to this stage, be very aware that you are weighing up the position as much as they are weighing up giving it to you. Don't be afraid to ask difficult, searching questions. After all, you need to get a real feel for how the board behaves. Is there a culture of openness and authenticity? The other IDs are morally obligated to give you detailed answers, even if the questions are uncomfortable.

This is your prime opportunity to do your due diligence on how the board *really* operates. Does the board truly value diversity and welcome different perspectives? Is the executive open to challenge, or are they playing lip service to compliance and then going off to do as they please?

The type of questions you might ask include:
- How would you describe the strategic priorities?
- How do you feel about the direction of strategy overall?
- What are the most crucial decisions the board is expecting to make over the next 12 months?
- What are the top three opportunities/challenges the organisation is facing in the short- or medium-term?
- How would you describe the relationship between the board and the chairperson/CEO?
- How does the CFO get on with chair?

If the answer to any of these questions elicits a mumbled, evasive response, this should rightly raise some red flags. Likewise, if the answers are not particularly full or focussed, this may indicate a lack of direction or communication amongst the current board members.

If you do not get offered the role you interview for, don't get disheartened. Appointments for IDs are not meritocratic. While skills are increasingly important, boards are also focussed on good fit. As discussed previously, this might mean balancing some more outspoken members with some that are more measured in their approach. Alternatively, the board might have had something very specific in mind.

NHS selection process

The assessment of ID candidates does vary sector by sector. In fact, the interview stage when applying to join the board of an NHS Trust frequently occurs over multiple stages. Again, you are advised to prepare well beforehand and to do some background reading and research to discover specific challenges. Useful sources of information can be found in Appendix E.

Make contact with the chair of the trust before you apply to get an understanding of the trust's priorities and the skills they are looking for. Contact details will be provided in the information packs you will receive from the trust. He or she should be willing to have an informal conversation to see whether this is the right role for you. You should also consider engaging with healthcare and local community networks to both raise your profile and get a greater understanding of the NHS and the various challenges it faces.

Applications are long-listed before they are passed to trust panels for consideration. In some cases, the trust will employ search consultants who will interview the long-listed applicants. Feedback will then be provided to the trust panel, which decides the candidates who are then invited in for an interview.

A formal interview process will follow, which will ask the usual questions about skills and expertise and how they'd apply to the particular role. There may also be an invitation to join in on any one of a series of meet-the-stakeholder type sessions.

In an 'open session', candidates are invited in for a session of about one to two hours, in which the chair of the trust and others outline the role and discuss the particular organisation and its strategy. It is a good opportunity for candidates to decide whether or not they are suitable for the role they've applied for before getting too far into the process. The session is not an assessment, and a potential candidate's performance at the event will not form part of the selection process.

If the trust in question is recruiting for a chair, there might be an informal interview with the chief executive over a breakfast or lunch. This is an opportunity for the trust board chief executive to meet candidates on an informal basis. Again, this is not a formal part of the recruitment process. The chief executive will be accountable to the chair, so it is not appropriate that they are responsible for making the decision about who to recruit. Indeed, chief executives do not take part in the interviews in this case. This informal session is more about getting a feel for someone as an individual.

Another option to be aware of is a carousel interview, which is designed to see how applicants respond and interact with the various stakeholders. Carousel attendees are typically drawn from a number of different stakeholder groups, such as staff, governors, service users and carers. Each group is managed by another trust board member and asked to focus on a particular section of the position's specification in order to assess the candidate in discussions that last around 30 minutes. Feedback is based on a narrative format rather than any sort of specific ranking for each candidate.

In another stage, candidates might be asked to preside over a meeting of trust IDs and governors as a chairperson. They are given a scenario in advance so they can plan how they will work through the scenario in a meeting situation. The trust will be looking out for how efficiently the candidate chairs the meeting, the strategic and economic decisions they lead it to, and whether or not they are able to process large amounts of information efficiently. Once again, narrative feedback is provided on the candidate's performance.

Two further activities which might be included are stakeholder presentations and focus group discussions. For the stakeholder presentations, candidates are asked to present a talk on a specific topic and then respond to questions from the stakeholders who have been invited to listen. A focus group discussion, as it implies, takes a group discussion format and is therefore more flexible. A number of issues are liable to be raised, under the direction of a facilitator, with the group allowed to pose open questions and create discussion topics.

Clearly, not all of these processes will be deployed for a single position. There is a balance to be struck between over-elaborate processes, which might put many potential applicants off, and finding the best person for the job. It is, however, useful to be aware of the varied methods of assessment.

Charitable trusts, sporting boards and university councils

In terms of advice for interview, I would say:

– Be clear on what you offer. If you can't articulate it well, it makes it very hard for the panel to choose you. Understanding where you might fit in and being honest about your strengths and weaknesses helps the interview team know if you are the right candidate for them.

– Be proactive. Research the organisation and speak to people within and around it, as it shows interest, diligence and shapes your understanding of the key issues which is useful for questions of the panel. Many people forget that it is a two-way interview process: If there isn't a cultural fit, it could be a very unhappy experience, so take the time to fully explore the opportunity and the time requirements needed to do it well.

– Be you! Don't try to second-guess what they are looking for or try to be anything that you are not, because a forward-thinking board will be looking for something different. A long time ago when I first joined Sport England's Regional Sports Board, I had a mentoring session with Baroness Karren Brady (a great inspiration and role model to me), and one of her biggest pieces of advice to me was to always be myself no matter what. A few years later I met the incredible Jayne Ashworth OBE, co-founder of StreetGames and I started noticing that the female directors I was inspired by were authentic and stayed true, despite the environment. I didn't fully appreciate it at the time, but I do now. It is too tempting at first to be 'magnolia' to blend into the background and 'fit in', but that is not why we are appointed as IDs. This is particularly in the case where you are brought in to help modernise a board. It is critical that you remain true to yourself and your values.

After all of this, take your time when making your final decision. With one of my appointments, to Warwickshire CCC, the recruitment process took a very long time and was quite involved. When the offer eventually came, there was a real sense of urgency their end. They'd made their decision and were ready to go. At this stage, I made sure to slow things down so I could do my own proper due diligence. I had to take a step back to make absolutely sure I was doing the right thing for myself and my career.

Michelle Leavesley, ID Warwickshire CCC, Sport & Play Construction Association, British Wheelchair Basketball

Since positions on charitable trusts, sporting boards and University Councils are generally unpaid, equal weight is often given to selling the charity/sport to the candidate, as much as the candidate selling himself or herself during the interview process. Indeed, the recruitment process could even start with an informal open day, where the organisation opens its doors and makes the chair and chief executive available to answer more questions about the organisation, its work and the existing board.

Interviewing may begin as a formal process, similar to the one everyone is familiar with for staff recruitment. CVs are submitted, a shortlist is drawn up and one-to-one interviews are conducted. (See previous sections for advice on how to prepare for interviews like this.) The process may then move into a more informal style, where candidates are invited to observe a board meeting and meet with existing IDs.

If the organisation is a membership organisation, the final decision may be made by the members. Candidate biographies will be circulated to each member ahead of the Annual General Meeting, alerting the members to the role, skills and attributes required. The selection is then put to the vote.

There is something very particular about the position of working through other people, which is what you will find yourself doing on a board. The skills I would look for are judgement and trust. There also needs to be real analytical capabilities to take on large, complex sets of data and make sense of them. Equally importantly is respect: People need to listen to those who hold different values and respect the difference.

Helen Baker, Current charity trustee roles include Shelter and The What Works Centre for Wellbeing

Confirming the appointment

If you get the role that you have applied for, congratulations! Following the confirmation, you may receive a Letter of Appointment, rather than a conventional contract. This will lay out the amount of time you will serve, the time commitment required, and location of board meetings. It will also set out details of any board committee posts you will hold and the fees (if any) you will be paid. It is quite likely that the organisation making the appointment will also take the opportunity to set out the aims of the board and to emphasise the legal responsibilities of the new ID, as well as the evaluation process for IDs.

Any new ID will be expected to register any business interests other than those of the company they are about to join, whether as a shareholder, director, officer, employee or trustee. If the company in question is listed on the Stock Market, the Letter of Appointment will reinforce the ID's responsibilities, should they hold shares in the company. Buying and selling of shares is liable to strict rules, which will be set out in that company's constitution and also via city regulations on listing requirements and insider trading laws.

Clauses in the Letter of Appointment will vary according to sector. Those joining an NHS Trust will be reminded that they are not allowed to make political speeches concerning the health service, or engage in other political activities. Similarly, the question of conflict of interest will be raised. New IDs are asked to declare any business interests, or positions of authority in a charity or voluntary body in the health sector, or any connection with businesses contracting for NHS services.

Appointees to charitable trust boards can also expect copies of the organisation's Articles of Association, rules or bylaws, as well as the charity's conflicts of interest policy, in addition to the basic terms such as length of appointment, dates of meeting and so on. If the charity is claiming gift aid, there is a requirement that trustees, as managers of the charity, pass the 'fit and proper persons' test. HMRC guidance will therefore be added to the letter, along with a declaration that the new ID has read and understood the guidance, which needs to be signed and returned.

If the role is with a smaller organisation, such as a community group, sports club or school, there will most likely be nothing like this level of formality. There will, however, always be some sort of an agreement to sign.

After the new ID has signed and returned the Letter of Appointment and any additional documentation or declaration as required, arrangements are made for the induction, or onboarding process.

Chapter 9
Advice for first-time independent directors

Michelle Leavesley was one of the first ever IDs on the board of British Wheelchair Basketball. The appointment came in the wake of the London Olympic and Paralympic Games in 2012, as part of a UK Sport requirement for National Governing Bodies of Sport to appoint independent NEDs. The transition, as she recalls, was not an easy one.

'The first few board meetings felt very uncomfortable. It was almost like we had gate crashed a private party!' she said. 'The elected board members probably wondered how we could contribute without any technical knowledge of the sport and the agenda lasted all day with lengthy conversations about detail such as team selections.'

'What we saw at British Wheelchair Basketball were lot of individuals working really hard, but they didn't have the synergy of a robust collective strategy and needed to create a sustainable future. As IDs our role was to help structure the board, to shape a strategy and think more commercially to create more sustainable revenue opportunities. We also started to put some of the performance measures in place to ensure that everyone was working collaboratively to build the future together.'

Michelle, who has now held four ID roles, as well as her 'day job' with M&G PLC as a Director of Organisational Risk & Resilience, says she has seen some progress in the perception of the role of IDs and what they can offer. There is now, she says, an acceptance that it is more than simply fulfilling a requirement of the Corporate Governance Code. There is an understanding that the role is value-adding and about helping a board to achieve the right strategic outcomes. Executives are also seeing the benefit of having independent IDs to call on as objective sounding boards outside the boardroom, providing a great mentoring and development opportunity for all.

While progress is being made, there are still the occasional misunderstandings and misconceptions that IDs need to deal with. In Michelle's case, she has found that not everyone is completely onboard with embracing the merits of diversity. Another of her board roles was as the second female board director appointment in a First Class County Cricket Club (Warwickshire CCC), which she credits to the forward-thinking of the chair, Norman Gascoigne, who took active measures to tackle what was widely seen as the 'male, pale and stale' environment in cricket. Unfortunately, not everyone was as broadminded. As she approached her table at an early cricket dinner, Michelle was mistaken as the Maitre' D and was asked for more bread rolls and butter.

'To this day people still joke about it, but it highlighted the assumption that a female in that environment (and in a suit) could only be present in that capacity rather than as a director,' Michelle said.

https://doi.org/10.1515/9783110706123-009

Other instances of unconscious bias are less amusing.

'I have also sat in an interview for a CEO where one of the candidates thought that, of the panel of three, I must be the note-taker,' she went on. 'He not only failed to say hello to me, but then turned his chair to face away from me, towards my colleagues. Not surprisingly, he was unsuccessful in his application.'

'It's not unheard of for people to reference me (or other female directors) as 'the quota'. This is particularly frustrating when you have been an ID for over 10 years, long before the idea of a quota was ever even raised.'

In Michelle's opinion, the boardroom behaviours required to be a success as an ID start with an openness to ideas that might feel uncomfortable from one's own personal experience of what might be the norm. The other absolute essentials are behavioural skills such as excellent listening skills, the ability to check and challenge effectively (with 'effectively' being the key) and having the courage to stand up for good governance when it matters.

She adds, 'The good news is that, when starting out, a good chair and board colleagues will help guide new recruits. It is therefore important that, when the 'L' plates are on, new IDs are open to learning and being mentored through their induction.'

One of the key characteristics you need to bring with you, and keep, is an open mind. In one organisation I joined, I assumed that I was brought in because of my knowledge of member-based organisations and HR experience. As it turned out, there was little need for my contribution there. The organisation was looking at two propositions: one was being acquired by another organisation and the other was a merger. There were many people there who had been there for some time, so they were not necessarily at an advantage when it came to the proposals, since they had very strong views either way. Since I had come in quite recently with an entirely open mind, I could afford to be neutral. I was able to compare and contrast without having invested feelings of my own. I wasn't making the final decision, but I was able to give valuable input towards that decision and help everyone else better consider all the variables.

Devyani Vaishampayan, Managing Partner, HR TECH Partnership

Joining a board is not simply a case of turning up and slotting in. There are many dynamics that come into play here, and getting them right sets an ID up for everything that comes next. The ultimate aim is for alignment between the IDs and the executive, which is incredibly powerful, particularly when you consider that the opposite scenario can be responsible for destroying an organisation. How that process is handled by both sides is crucial.

Alignment doesn't mean that IDs have to say yes to everything executives put forward in order to fit in and not rock the boat. This is something you often see in dysfunctional boards where IDs and the executive operate in parallel to one another. In other words, the executives treat board meetings as something to endure. They'll give a few presentations, allow a few questions and then depart to do exactly what they had been intending to do in the first place. This far-from-satisfactory situation is enabled when IDs meekly adopt the role of some sort of observer who will provide a modicum of insight but, other than that, will keep their distance.

There is another type of unaligned and dysfunctional board which is just as dangerous as the ineffective one. This is where there is no clear division between the executives and non-executive roles. Everyone is trying to run the show and show off their strategic savvy. There is no clear division between anyone's jobs. The result? A complete mess where, most likely, nothing gets accomplished.

For a board to be effective and work constructively, everyone needs to know and understand their respective roles and give each other space and encouragement to achieve theirs. This is not to say there will never be a certain amount of creative tension and dissent. There will be, and that's important too. Just as important, an ID needs to have a deep understanding of the organisation they are joining. While it is quite likely they were chosen because of previous relevant industry or sector experience, they also need to understand the very specific nuances around the board they are now part of. It is only by getting fully to grips with every aspect of the organisation, from the management team, to the culture, to the product/service, to the customer, that can IDs truly be of value.

But how do you achieve this happy medium? It's not an easy thing to do, particularly if you are new to being an ID. The best start to achieving this ideal is via thorough 'onboarding', or induction, programmes which are run over several days prior to an ID taking up their new boardroom position. In an ideal world, no new ID would simply be thrown in at the deep end to sink or swim. Sadly though, IDs need to be prepared that this formal onboarding process is not always on offer. Despite the increased scrutiny of boardroom behaviour, as well as a greater willingness to enhance the diversity of the boardroom by encouraging applications from a range of backgrounds and experiences, too many boards appear to have resisted the increased pressure to put more effort into successfully integrating new members. The take-up of onboarding as an accepted formal process has been painfully slow. Research shows that 31% of corporate boards do not have formal induction programmes,[1] and 24% of directors said they were responsible for their own onboarding. Many boards offer only limited, generic induction programmes too. These figures are for FTSE 350 companies. While the equivalent data for voluntary boards such as charities, sporting organisations and universities is hard to come by, evidence from a recent Henley Business School study[2] appears to show that onboarding is even less common in these sectors. The downside to a lack of onboarding arrangements, whatever the sector, is that without them, it can take many months for a new director to feel effective on the board, or, indeed, able to make their mark.

Before we tackle what any new ID can do to help themselves quickly get up to speed, if a formal onboarding programme is not on offer, let's just look at the ideal case scenario. This is what *should* happen.

Responsibility for overseeing onboarding arrangements is frequently delegated to the nominations committee, and the actual programme is then run by the company secretary or equivalent role, depending upon the sector. Ideally, the chairperson and CEO should be fully involved in the induction too. The goal is that new board members are given all they need in order to take an active role and contribute from the start. The materials and briefings that should be made available to the new ID include:

- Insights on any public and policy disclosures.
- Access to non-publicised materials, such as minutes from previous board meetings, forecasts, budgets and strategic plans.
- Biographies of key executives and the senior management team.

In addition, meetings will be set up on both a formal and informal basis with the executive team and relevant senior managers. This is hugely helpful in getting to know more about boardroom dynamics and culture, as well as the different perspectives of an ID's new colleagues. A breakfast or dinner meeting, or even just a coffee, with new colleagues is always well worth it and will pay dividends in the long run. It'll give you context you wouldn't get any other way and certainly more than simply relying on briefing notes. Site visits may be arranged, where applicable.

Occasionally, some larger boards may offer some general training in the role of a board and on the responsibilities of individual directors, as well as on relevant governance regulations. Some sort of mentoring programme might also be on offer, which is also very welcome, particularly for first-time board members. This allows new IDs to build helpful relationships while at the same time learning from more experienced members of the board. These opportunities are, however, quite rare in some sectors. It may well be something a keen new ID might consider taking on for themselves.

Whether or not an organisation is switched on to provide onboarding, or offers any sort of welcome process at all, IDs should recognise that getting up to speed with their new position is a two-way process. It stands to reason that a new ID fully engages with the management committee and its way of doing things, and it bodes pretty badly if they don't. In addition to the materials provided by the board, it is generally expected that a new ID does their own research to get to grips with the following areas that will have an impact on the organisation they are starting work with:

- Any public disclosures, internet references, regulatory filings and governance documents including corporate governance principles.
- Desk research on industry and competitor trends.

- Specific governance issues affecting the sector as a whole.
- Any broader study programmes that might supplement an understanding of governance issues, director responsibilities and factors concerning the sector.

It is quite likely that a diligent ID would have done a lot of research in this direction as part of their due diligence ahead of the first interview. Now it is time to take a deeper dive into the issues and develop a fuller understanding of the organisation and its aims, as well as its position in its sector. All of this is done with the understanding that, no matter how many papers you read, there is no substitute for meeting and talking with fellow directors. This is the time when IDs begin to really understand an organisation and its culture.

This entire process does, of course, take time. Fortunately, boards are increasingly selecting new IDs far enough in advance of the official start date to allow for this preparation. There may even be opportunities for shadowing of board and committee meetings. I've known some boards operate as much as a year in advance, but, as always, there are stragglers. Many new IDs report attending their first board meeting within a month of being appointed.

The final opportunity to get more fully acquainted with the board and its culture will occur at the dinner/breakfast that is often held ahead of the formal board meeting. This is always a great opportunity to build on informal relationships with other board members without being hamstrung by the strict boundaries of an agenda. IDs will learn that this is frequently the forum where IDs and executives float ideas that might not be quite ready to be discussed in the boardroom. It's a great opportunity for small talk.

So, after the preparation, formal or otherwise, what can an ID expect from their first board meeting? They should receive board briefing papers which are sent out to all directors, usually at least a few days in advance of the actual meeting. The board papers should be well presented and comprehensive, but not so long and detailed as to be unreadable. Clearly, every director is best advised to read the papers, not only so they are up to speed with what will be discussed, but also for compliance reasons. If things later break apart, it is no defence for an ID to say that they didn't have time to read everything. The reason for sending the papers out in advance, in addition to the fact it gives everyone time to consume them, is so that board members have enough time to request any additional material if required.

Following your due diligence/onboarding and perusal of board papers, you should be familiar with most of what is going on at the organisation right now. You'll also have met with the executive and non-executive teams. Even so, it would be a confident person indeed who did not feel the pressure of walking into a room full of people they don't know that well, armed only with several hundred pages of detailed information about an organisation. All the while you'll be aware that you are expected to make decisions that will ensure its future success in just a few short hours. (Oh, and if success doesn't follow, you will be accountable.)

The first thing I would say to anyone is to believe in yourself and your ability. If you don't believe in yourself, no one else will. As scary as it is walking into a boardroom, or similar situation for the first time, don't think about it that way. Put your shoulders back, hold your head up high, and look everyone in the eye and say, 'I'm here'. It doesn't matter if you are bricking it on the inside. On the outside, you have to exude confidence.

I was very lucky to have a good mentor who told me to listen well and then to think very carefully about what questions you ask. If you ask some very valid questions, people will begin to take notice. The timing of your question is important too. Likewise, if you think someone is bullshitting, call them out on it. Be careful how you frame it, though. Say something like: *Can you tell me the possible outcome of what it is you are saying? I am not sure I understand.* If they are just speaking because they like the sound of their own voice, they won't be able to reply without bullshitting some more.

My absolute rule is to never pick an argument unless I absolutely know all the facts. That's the only way to be effective.

Most of all, stick to your core values and beliefs. There is nothing worse than seeing other people sitting there like nodding dogs, when they clearly don't agree with what's being discussed. They just want others in the room to think they are all over the subject, when they really don't need to behave that way. It's fine to sit still and give nothing away with your body language and then pose your really relevant question at the right time.

Janie Frampton, Executive Chair and Head of International Relations at International Socca Federation, Director, Sports Officials Consultancy, Patron, Muslim Women's Network UK

First-time IDs may find their initial board meeting vastly different from their usual experience of meetings back in the 'real' world. Boards have a comparatively short amount of time to discuss some often complex issues. This frequently leads to extensive discussions which may head off several different avenues without apparently getting any closer to a satisfactory outcome. It is the role of the chair to steer the conversation, ascertain the various views around the table and to make sure each view is explored properly. The ultimate aim is, of course, to finish the meeting with a coherent set of ideas for the senior management to go away and execute efficiently.

If the organisation is run well, it is likely that the chair will have reached out to other board members ahead of the meeting and, in particular, the new IDs to discuss the agenda. The idea of these prior conversations is to bring any concerns to the surface now that the board has read the advance papers. Knowing what the issues are will help the chair to structure the conversation on the day and make sure everyone has a say. The last thing that anyone wants or needs is for a debate to float aimlessly around the room. The chair should have planned landmarks to keep it on track, while ensuring the discussion is sufficient to cover the subject in the depth it deserves. You may find the chair summing up the conversation periodically, which is part of the process of keeping things moving along.

Board meetings sometimes begin with the CEO, or equivalent role, addressing the room with what will be covered that day. This is his/her opportunity to talk about the major issues that are having an impact on the organisation since the board last met and highlight what may be coming up between that meeting and the next one. Depending on the sector, they may briefly give a political overview of what is happening in the country, such as a proposal to raise taxes, or a change in legislation which might have an impact. What is happening at a customer/service user level might also come up, particularly if there are any significant changes, such as a shift in users, or a significant response to a new product/service either from your organisation or a competitor. It is a holistic view, which gives the board context for what is to follow.

The board will then move on to running through the information in the package that had previously been sent out. There will be someone on hand to take notes to record actions for follow-ups on each point. This is essential, since board members often volunteer in the enthusiasm of the moment, and think, 'Oh, I'll make that introduction,' or 'I'll do this', but may need to be reminded to complete the tasks later on. An email will be sent out after the meeting with a list of follow-up tasks, defining who is tied to which particular action task. This may be separate from board minutes that will also be sent out for approval.

A critical part of every board meeting is a review of the finances, which is generally presented by the CFO. He/she may not be going through the P&L line by line. That information may well have already been presented in the board briefing notes, along with a summary of the year-to-date performance. This is the opportunity for the board to ask searching questions about the financials. No board should be in a position where the IDs just accept being spoon fed the numbers and then the proceedings rapidly move on. By the same token, if all appears well, and the tough questions are answered satisfactorily, the meeting should move on. If too long is spent looking backward, it reduces the time available to move strategy forward.

Equally important to the agenda will be whatever issue is keeping the CEO (or equivalent) awake at night, because there is almost always a significant challenge facing any organisation. They may have prepared a white paper outlining the issue, with any relevant background, and the discussion about the challenge may well take up to an hour or more of the board meeting as a strategy is developed.

Another common component of a board meeting is director education. This is where someone from within the business is invited in to make a presentation. It might be someone senior from, for example, marketing, HR, or distribution, and they will be asked to do a deep dive into what they do and why it is an important part of the organisation. Alternatively, an expert from outside the organisation, such as an entrepreneur, academic, writer or consultant, will be brought in to give new insights into the industry or relevant subjects. This is all hugely important to developing the boardroom's insight into various parts of the business. Often, it will spark new perspectives and might even prompt ID to jump in and offer their own angle on the subject, thanks to their personal area of expertise. The discussions that this generates will materially add to an organisation's understanding of a particular issue and be subsequently reflected in the execution of future strategy.

The structure of each board meeting will vary, but there are various other components that will come up over the year. There should be regular budget and strategy reviews, where it is the ID's role to vet the plans set by management and agree a consensus on the way forward. Reviews of products and services should be another regular, as an organisation makes sure that it is on track for both today and tomorrow. Again, an ID is well-placed to play a key role here, since they are not bogged down with thinking about these things in terms of the day-to-day performance. They'll be able to take a helicopter view, pinpointing threats and opportunities well into the future. There may also be a review of an organisation's position in relation to competitors, particularly if there are significant shifts in the market afoot. Likewise, what new developments in technology are emerging? Other subjects that might periodically come up for discussion include expansion in the area of new products or services, as well as geographic, any major capital investments, and compensation strategies. Finally, there will be regular scrutiny of the organisational structure. People come and go, and it is crucial to make sure that the right people are in the right place, now and in the future. This applies in particular to the succession plan for key roles such as the CEO or chair.

Separately from the board meeting, there may also be a need to attend a stand-alone executive session, certainly for IDs with public companies, but this is becoming more common in organisations elsewhere. This is where IDs meet alone without the CEO, or equivalent, and the rest of the executive team. The chair will head these meetings and it is an excellent opportunity to discuss strategy or any highly sensitive topics. This may be where an ID might put forward a proposal about selling off a certain division, for example. This is never an easy thing to raise in front of an executive who may be working night and day to resolve any issues at the said division. Likewise, this is the forum to raise any concerns about the performance of executives. Feedback will then be consolidated and provided to the executive team.

In either scenario, whether it is a full board meeting, or a stand-alone executive session, this might seem like quite a daunting agenda. First-time directors might assume that they should listen more than talk during their first few meetings. The thought process might be that they are better off observing the board and getting to know its dynamics before making a contribution. This is not actually recommended. IDs should certainly be prepared to participate in the discussion. IDs are there for a reason: to add value. Yes, it is correct that the CEO and executives are likely to have more detailed and up-to-date knowledge than IDs, but the value an ID gives is being able to step back and see the broader picture, as well as digging into the details when necessary.

It's challenging to be the newbie, but there are advantages too. You can see things with a fresh pair of eyes and people are more forgiving when you ask what might feel like a naive question, but actually turns out to be quite pertinent. It's also a lot easier to question decisions which were made before you were there, and are therefore not your decisions. Being new can be quite a positive thing.

Jane Chafer, Various ID positions including Plymouth Argyle,
Sheffield International Venues, FX Plus

New IDs will quickly get a feel for when to contribute and when to stay quiet. In fact, there are three strategies open to them, as articulated so succinctly in the title of the book *Boards that Lead: When to Take Charge, When to Partner and When to Stay Out of the Way.*[3] Here, the message is that when an organisation is developing strategy, setting out risk, *partnership* with the executive team is of utmost importance. Conversely, during periods of smooth sailing and steady growth, an ID should largely stay out of the way. When it comes to selecting a new chair or CEO, or reacting when there is a crisis, or a question of ethics, IDs need to step in and take charge.

The absolute rule is to be sure that you have done all the background reading ahead of the meeting so that when you do speak, you do so from a position of knowledge. This includes absorbing the board calendar that you'll be provided with, which will show the activities and priorities in the coming months, over and above the first meeting you are attending. Thus, you won't fall into any obvious beartraps, such as wondering out loud why the board isn't discussing the budgetary aspect of a particular decision, when in reality it is scheduled to be talked about at the next board meeting. Likewise, don't try to make your mark early on by wading in and immediately beginning to point out where an organisation is going wrong. To be effective, trust needs to be built and, while there is a need to quickly get up-to-speed with everything, this won't happen overnight. Yes, an ID is there to challenge the executive, but you need to know that you are on the right track. This means you need to try and get a feel for the boardroom dynamics and culture before you make bold pronouncements.

The cultures of organisations do vary considerably, and that will often have a lot to do with the way they are structured. Jane Chafer, who has been an ID across a number of sporting organisations, has some interesting insight into this.

'My first ID role was on the board of Sheffield International Venues, a not-for-profit leisure trust with the aim of inspiring people to be active and use some of the great sporting facilities in the city. It was very commercial on one level, but also very much about the community. No one person owned the company and all of the money made was reinvested. It was very fast-paced because they had a lot they wanted to do and they were open to all ideas.'

'A football club can be very different. Generally, there will be a chairman who might have invested tens of millions of their own money into making it a success. Yes, the CEO is running things, but the chairman clearly has a presence. I know that when I joined Plymouth Argyle, I thought: *I am going to advise the chairman and say what I think, but if he wants to take a particular action, that has to be his prerogative*. As it was, there has been a culture of totally active discussion.

'Our current chair (Simon Hallett), for example, is very open and very transparent. He is very happy to take advice, and keen to hear other people's views. There are often strong differences of opinion around the board about something that we've put forward. The chair is amenable to changing his mind about what he wants to do, or will invite more information because someone has said something from an angle that others haven't thought about.'

Communication skills are key. IDs need to perfect a style of speaking that influences without being dictatorial. When you speak, think carefully about the way you couch your contribution. Take your time to educate and persuade. This entails being able to articulate complex ideas in a clear, yet engaging way. The aim is that an ID enlightens boardroom colleagues to their areas of expertise, advising on a range of issues in a helpful, non-judgemental manner. Most important, you need to take your colleagues with you. You will only manage this by adding something useful to the mix, fully committing yourself to the process and by being consistent. This is the way to build a reputation that you can be proud of and to contribute something valuable, which is why you signed up in the first place.

When you are weighing up when to speak and what to say, it's worth reminding yourself that your job as an ID is not simply to catch out wrongdoing or potential problems. You are also there to support the CEO and his or her executive team. It's a cliché, but life at the top can be pretty lonely sometimes. There is a lot of responsibility that goes with running an organisation of any size, particularly in a tough economic climate. People are quick to criticise and point their finger, but it is less common for them to praise top management for a job well done. IDs should make a point of being supportive when things are going well and finding something they like to complement the executive about.

If you do find yourself in a situation where you have genuine concerns, consider carefully how you couch your questions about the issue. The delivery is as important as the question itself. If a question is phrased in a clumsy or hostile way, everyone else in the room will be bristling with indignation, particularly if you are the new boy or girl. This is hardly conducive to a measured response from your new boardroom colleagues. Think in terms of framing questions about the issue in an open-ended way. Try 'How are you thinking about . . .', rather than the more aggressive 'Have you considered . . .' Avoid declarative statements that show you have completely discounted the subject under discussion.

Any ID who does, even for a fleeting moment, feel out of their depth should be aware that the onus is on the chairman to make it work. It is up to them to create the culture and dynamic to extract the maximum value from each board member and ensure multiple voices are heard in board discussions. Any experienced chair worth their salt will understand that the newest member of the board will need a little help to get settled in and find their stride.

I've served on a board where the chair pushed things through and rolled his eyes whenever anyone raised a query. It doesn't work. I've tried very hard not create an environment like that because the role of the chair is hugely important, particularly in terms of how everyone's voice is heard. I know that it's not always easy to speak up and question things, especially when everyone else on the board seems to be nodding along and saying, 'Yes, yes, yes, everything is fine.'

I often say to people that if they feel like their concerns are not coming across, they should speak to me independently either before the meeting or afterwards. I also try to make sure everyone speaks during meetings. Sometimes you have to find different ways to do this. We held a half day meeting where there was no agenda. Everybody could ask what they wanted and give their views. That worked well. Occasionally, we also have meetings with just the independent directors present. It means they can stop pretending and express their frustrations – that's pretty good.

Sarah Turvill, Chair of Council, University of Exeter

Fellow board members should also be supportive. Accept their help when offered and don't be afraid to say when you have a question on something. You will have gaps in your knowledge to begin with. That is to be expected. By definition, a new board member will lack perspective on the board's history. They won't know all of the issues that have been debated and argued over ad nauseam already. Understand that there is a balance here. A fresh perspective can move things out of a rut, but it can also rehash old arguments and risk pushing the board into another unproductive cul de sac. (This is also why it is important to have read the board minutes going back for the previous year or so, so you have some understanding of the recurring key issues and debates.)

New IDs should also not feel left in the dark when it comes to their performance in the initial meeting or meetings. It's good practice to take the chair aside afterwards and ask, *How did I do?* The chair may well offer his or her view unprompted. They might respond that you did well and that they were pleased with the points you made. If, on the other hand, they say you spoke too much and took up too much time, take the comments on board and consider if the chair had a point. If you agree, adjust your behaviour next time. There is no substitute for these honest one-to-one conversations when it comes to understanding and appreciating boardroom dynamics. Apart from anything else, it means everyone feels more comfortable as and when potentially controversial topics come up. No one will be reluctant to speak, which is as it should be.

Not all boards are the same. Many will be run on a less dynamic or formal basis. This book has focussed on a range of different type of appointments and, not surprisingly, the way boardrooms function will vary depending on the sector. There will occasionally be frustrations about getting things done. However, just because it is difficult to make significant changes, this does not mean you should switch off. Perseverance is key.

> While you need to focus on areas where you know you can make a difference. That doesn't mean you should ignore the other areas. I would certainly keep up the questions.
> **Dipti Amin, Independent Director, Cambridge Innovation Capital,**
> **University of Hertfordshire, Buckinghamshire Healthcare Trust**

Something that new IDs might encounter – particularly when joining smaller, voluntary boards – is they may well find themselves as the most experienced person in the room, particularly if they come from a business background and are used to working in that sort of environment. Perhaps the board position has only recently been formalised, after a period where the governing body was run by members of the organisation who perhaps played sport for a club, or have some other sort of close association with it. A board that's made up of enthusiastic amateurs who may have been in place for some time will present a not insubstantial challenge. The goal is, of course, to create a check and challenge culture. This is where everyone is involved in the conversation, not just the loudest voice in the room, and everyone's view is taken on board. A new way of doing business will need to be introduced where all members are expected, even obligated, to ask questions, engage in a purposeful dialogue and pose challenges rather than simply rubber-stamping all suggestions.

The big question that every new ID should always bear in mind when they first join any board, regardless of its size, is: *How do I have an impact?* They will have made a significant personal and professional commitment by signing up to be an ID and will naturally want to make it count. If you have been brought in thanks to a particular area of expertise, such as technology, or international experience, or product development, the way forward will be clear. There will be a call to advise on specific strategies in the sector, mentor fellow board members and perhaps make useful introductions. Elsewhere, use the skills you have learned through your career to begin having an impact. This was why you were recruited in the first place. Prepare yourself for the fact that fellow directors will probe you about your views and will ask challenging questions. That's all fine, and is a good sign that you are making a difference.

Notes

1 https://www.russellreynolds.com/insights/thought-leadership/accelerating-board-impact-for-new-directors, November 2015.
2 https://assets.henley.ac.uk/defaultUploads/research/Research-Report-The-Role-of-Non-Executive-Directors-in-Growth-Companies.pdf?mtime=20190904142950
3 Ram Charan, Dennis Carey and Michael Useem, *Boards that lead: When to take charge, when to partner and when to stay out of the way*. Harvard Business Review Press, December 2013.

Chapter 10
Troubleshooting

Sir Peter Thompson has an interesting story to tell. He made his name and reputation when he led the flotation of the former state-owned transport company National Freight Corporation (NFC) in 1989. He'd joined the sprawling state-owned company in 1948, when it was heavily burdened with debt, and transformed it entirely by consolidating its various off-shoots and focusing on the profitable segments of the organisation. What made his strategy all the more remarkable for its time was the innovative employee share-ownership scheme which made more than 10,000 workers and pensioners considerably better off after they invested £6.1 million in shares.

With Peter being dubbed the 'grandfather of the management buyout' in the press in various breathlessly complementary articles, he must have seemed like an obvious choice to invite onto the board of British & Commonwealth, another sprawling company which had had somewhat of a chequered history. British & Commonwealth had suffered from many of the ups and downs that plagued NFC since it was established in 1955, when Clan Line Steamers was merged with Union Castle to form the British & Commonwealth Shipping Company. Various other businesses, from airlines, to helicopters, to containers, had been bolted on right up until the early 1980s. At this point, the new management under John Gunn had switched to financial services. A further rapid expansion led to the business being dubbed 'the largest financial services company in the UK' (barring the then Big Four high street banks). In 1988, in another change of direction, British & Commonwealth bought Atlantic Computers for £434 million.

When a couple of Peter's city contacts invited him to become an independent director, he was told there was not a great deal to it.

'They said it was a question of four board meetings a year, a bit of background reading and a nice dinner once a year,' Sir Peter recalls. 'I was persuaded that was not going to be difficult to fit in, even for a busy executive as I was at the time.'

The first board meeting was fairly standard. Sir Peter asked the usual questions about the business plans, dug into the results to date and discussed the acquisition of Atlantic. The answers that came back bothered him enough to demand an immediate audit of the computer services business. Something felt terribly wrong. Just to add to his concerns, John Gunn was very reluctant indeed to appoint auditors. When the results of the audit came through, Sir Peter's worst fears were realised. I'll let him take up the story.

'"*It's a total Ponzi company*," was what they said,' Sir Peter said. (A Ponzi scheme is a get-rich-quick pyramid scheme, where the people at the top get paid, but those further down always lose out.) 'Atlantic Computers had grown on the back of an offer that people paid for a five-year contract. Then, at the end of the five years, they could give up those contracts and get one of the next generation of

https://doi.org/10.1515/9783110706123-010

computers. That all worked like a charm. Well, as long as the next generation were more expensive than the previous generation. Of course, there came a time where this no longer worked. Computer technology started getting cheaper! People were coming in and getting the cheaper ones.'

Aware the company was in a potentially fatal position, Sir Peter was asked to become chairman to try to sort the mess out. Against his better judgement, he agreed. Sir Peter again:

'I think there was a little pride involved. Up until that moment, I had only ever had success. I thought, "*I can do this.*" Unfortunately, I couldn't.'

From being a four-meetings-a-year, soft option, the role exploded into a full-time job for six brutal weeks as Sir Peter and the rest of the board battled to save British & Commonwealth. The media got hold of the story and, sensing imminent disaster, pursued all the members of the board relentlessly. The question that was asked again and again was: Where were the board members when all this was happening? How could the independent directors have let the acquisition of Atlantic Computers pass when there was such an obvious black hole there? Eventually, despite the best efforts of the board, the business collapsed into administration. It was hugely damaging to the reputations of everyone involved.

'It is a very sobering experience to become involved in a business that is apparently sound and where the balance sheets seem fine, only to discover that nothing is further from the truth when you join a board,' Sir Peter warns. 'One of the toughest parts were the pieces in the FT, accusing the non-execs of lining their pockets when the company was on its knees. I managed to get an apology from them when I pointed out that the company actually owed me money. Even so, that was a reputation downgraded.'

Sadly, the British & Commonwealth episode was not the only ID role that bothered Sir Peter and made him question how the system works. The outcome of another appointment, while nowhere near as final as the British & Commonwealth experience, left him feeling quite cynical about the power that IDs have to change things.

The story began with an invitation to join the board of Pilkington, the glass manufacturer with roots going back to 1826. Sir Peter was still at NFC at the time, but was sufficiently intrigued by the approach to agree. Although the company had made its name with the modern 'float' technique of glass-making, it had lost its way a little. However, it had recently successfully fought an unfriendly takeover bid by BTR Industries, another British conglomerate.

Shortly after Sir Peter joined, the issue of finding a replacement for the chief executive arose. The incumbent was on the brink of retirement, so a search needed to begin. Various names were put forward and discussed at a board meeting. One that the then chairman, Sir Anthony Pilkington, seemed particularly taken with was a character that had been on the management team for some decades. Sir Peter recalls that both he and Sir Roger Hurn, a fellow ID who was then an executive director at Smiths Industries, both raised an eyebrow at the suggestion. In their view, the suggested candidate was wholly unsuitable and, not only that, they felt uncomfortable that it was being presented as practically a done deal. Where was the due process? The pair voiced their opinions, but were not entirely convinced they were being listened to. Certainly, the other ID on the board showed very little reaction.

At the next board meeting, their worst fears were realised. At the dinner that was traditionally held ahead of the formal meeting, Sir Anthony breezily announced that his man had accepted the job.

'Here we see the classic non-executive dilemma,' Sir Peter says. 'The only real sanction that you really have is to sack the chief executive or chairman. No one else can do that. The alternative is to resign in protest. But you can only do that once.'

'That time at Pilkington's, we were new non-execs and probably a bit wet behind the ears, so we did nothing. It was a mistake because the company did really lose the plot. Since then, I've always made a point of asking non-executives what they think their role is. Invariably, they always come back with something along the lines of *helping with strategy* or *making sure the board abides by the rules*. I always respond that they have not addressed the one inescapable job of a non-executive, and that is to sack the chairman and chief executive if they are not up to the job. It's a daunting prospect, but that's the reality.'

—

It would be entirely remiss of any book exhorting the virtues of becoming an ID to not be entirely honest about the potential downsides. Sir Peter's experiences graphically illustrate that there can be real challenges that come with the role. Despite being a hugely respected and experienced business leader, he still suffered a real setback with one appointment and was disappointed in his performance at another. And, as we have seen, even though he was in a part-time role at British & Commonwealth and the damage was arguably done before he arrived, he still caught as much of the flack as the full-time executives.

The governance climate has changed since either of the appointments detailed here. There have been successive rules introduced to tighten up governance and a number of new codes. Yet, despite all of this, there are still behaviour obstacles to proper oversight. We know this because scandals are still happening today with depressing frequency.

If the management comes to the board with a proposal for something, board members have to be really careful about the way they challenge it. It's much, much better for everyone to see proposals at an early stage, before they're firm proposals, so that they can shape what's coming. Probing questions can be asked, which are also constructive. There can be good, tough discussions, without it becoming confrontational. If it gets to the stage where it is a challenge to management in the boardroom, then that is getting into the realms of saying, *I don't trust you. I don't think you're good enough and I don't agree with your proposal.* That can be quite a problem. A certain amount of diplomacy and etiquette is required.

Ruth Cairnie, Chair, Babcock International, Non-Executive, Rolls Royce, Associated British Foods and ContourGlobal

Aside from being willing to step up when the time comes and being willing to fire a chairman and chief executive, what other helpful advice can be given to a new ID, to help them stay out of harm's way? (And, equally important, stop their boards from hitting the buffers.) What are the warning signs that all is not well? What do you do when something comes up that you believe doesn't seem right? Or, worse still, looks blatantly wrong? What is the best way to approach it to find the best resolution for everyone and avoid alienating anyone (or yourself), which might jeopardise all future board activities?

The consensus of all the interviewees for this book is that the answers to these questions lie in a multi-stage process, which begins at the moment an ID signs up to their seat on the board. They need to convince other board members that they are fully engaged in the process and genuinely care for the organisation they are working with. Anyone who adopts the stance of simply turning up for their allotted hours and doing the bare minimum while they are there is unlikely to command the respect or attention of their peers. Whenever they do pipe up with their two penny-worth after deciding something is not quite right, their advice will most likely fall on deaf ears because others will, perhaps quite rightly, feel they have not fully invested in the organisation thus far. For any sort of questioning to work, there needs to be a strong relationship in the first place. Executives need to believe that IDs have invested the time to fully understand their perspective and that they therefore have skin in the game.

In a similar vein, putting in the time and going the extra mile will help an ID fully understand the culture of an organisation – in other words, how things are done around here. Understanding and immersing yourself into the board setting will pay dividends when it comes to how important points are raised when something needs to be said.

Having put in the groundwork, IDs are advised to take the following steps if and when something comes up that makes them feel uncomfortable.

Understand the background

How did the organisation arrive at this particular proposed course of action? It is highly likely that, by the time the subject is being discussed at board level, it has already been endlessly discussed and argued about by a number of people in the organisation. What is the history of this proposal? Why are they convinced that they have now got the right answer?

Plan your response

Jumping in and declaring that something is preposterous, or just plain wrong, won't win an ID many friends. In fact, it can make others on the board quite hostile to any further discourse. Likewise, declaring something along the lines of 'When this came up previously in my career, it was a disaster then too' is not a good way to challenge anything.

In the first instance, raise any concerns in a one-to-one conversation with the relevant executive that has presented the strategy.

Persist

Not diving in is not the same as remaining low-key. If one-to-one discussions with the relevant executive do not appear to be making any headway, or your concerns are not assuaged, take things to the next stage. Raise the issue with the chair of the board and carefully map out your arguments. The final stage is to take it to the whole board.

> The aim for an ID should always be to make boardroom colleagues feel like they are working alongside them, with the problem *in front* of you all, rather in judgement of them with the problem *between* you.
>
> One of my roles is on the board of the Centre for Data Ethics and Innovation (CDEI), the government regulator for artificial intelligence and data ethics in the UK. That board is full of luminaries, including Professor Lord Robert Winston, the geneticist, Right Reverend Dr. Steven Croft, Bishop of Oxford, Dame Patricia Hodgson, the former chair of OFCOM, and various other senior industry figures. I'm very much a younger figure on the board. While I know quite a lot about some things that the others don't, I am also conscious of my lack of experience.
>
> There was an occasion where the executive of the CDEI were pushing quite hard for a set of ethical principles and a code around fairness in the use of artificial intelligence. This was in response to criticism and concerns over the way some companies might be using algorithms to discriminate against genders, or particular ethnicities, in things like the pricing of car insurance or the recruitment of individuals.
>
> My viewpoint was that the world is not short of another set of principles or codes. Far more important is an understanding of how companies actually go about making these algorithms fair. The CDEI has a fantastic opportunity to distinguish itself from almost every other regulatory and advisory body by actually describing and setting down the operational practices that would allow businesses and organizations to do this.
>
> I knew that this would be quite countercultural for the civil servants who were working on this strategy. In order to land the message, I began by having some one-to-one chats with the chief exec of the body and a couple of others on the board. I wanted to make sure that they knew this was coming and that I didn't embarrass them in the board meeting. I also wanted to give them the confidence that there was another way through this. Just because it's something they didn't know about, it wasn't a threat to them. In fact, it was an opportunity. I was also able to put forward ideas for various recruitment opportunities, so we could hire people who had the expertise to make it happen.
>
> The aim was to provide an easy solution, rather than just giving them back a problem and saying, '*What you've done is not right, you need to do this.*' If I had just presented the bare bones of an idea, they'd have said, '*Well, how do we do that?*' As soon as people are unsure about how to move forward, their resistance will tend to grow. Nobody wants to look silly.
>
> **Richard Sargeant, Chief Commercial Officer, Faculty; ID, Exeter University;**
> **Government Centre for Data Ethics and innovation**

While it is important to always speak up, even if your opinion is not in the majority, choose your battles carefully. Not every issue will sit comfortably with your own personal values and beliefs, but that is not the point. You need to consider each issue in the context of its importance to the organisation in question. There is a lot of truth in the saying 'Sometimes you need to lose the battle to win the war'. If you consistently sweat the small stuff and get stuck on operational details, there is a danger that you lose impact when you come to the big stuff, the decisions which are really business critical. Understanding how and when to challenge is very important.

There will be some tough decisions to make and sometimes, IDs will have to make some uncomfortable interventions. But that is, at least partly, what they are there for. By the same token, IDs will have to accept that they will occasionally be put in some distressing situations. One of the most difficult situations that an ID will face is when there are allegations of wrongdoing by other members of the organisation. This will most likely mean that they have to take an active role in investigating it and, if found to be true, putting satisfactory sanctions in place.

One of the IDs interviewed for this book described just such a situation, where an outside regulator had become involved and approached them directly to ask them to investigate certain allegations.

'It was probably one of the toughest things I have ever had to do,' the ID explained. (We have not identified the source, at their request.) 'I received a call over the weekend which made the allegation about a senior member of staff and asked me to investigate immediately. We were given a very, very short timescale to report back. I had to go through a large amount of board papers and interview a number of people, which involved some fairly challenging conversations with people who may or may not be part of the problem. It wasn't just that that was difficult either. The other members of the board started to eye me suspiciously, because I was in charge of the investigation. It was all a big reality check about the responsibilities of an ID.'

An investigation like this would inevitably cause some tension on the board, at least in the short-term. What, though, if the board couldn't see eye-to-eye at all, over a long period? One of the worst things that can happen on a board is when there is a complete breakdown in relationships. Occasionally, some boards do find themselves in exactly this position, where the executives and IDs find it nearly impossible to get anything done. The rift between the various characters appears insurmountable.

What are the warning signs that such a rift is happening, and what causes it to all go wrong?

Let's start with the warning signs. One of the most common is conformity or groupthink. This is where the board has become so disillusioned by the whole process over a period of time that they are completely disinterested and say yes to everything. (This could also be a symptom of laziness, or social loafing. The idea is that there are enough other people on the board to do the heavy lifting, so why get too involved?) An alternative version is where people do have what may be valid alternative views but do not voice them for fear of being seen to differ from their colleagues. The result? When no one speaks up, mistake after mistake is made. You only need to revisit many of the boardroom scandals listed in Chapter 4 to see how dangerous groupthink can be.

Another clear red light is when boardroom relations break down to such an extent that the board fragments into factions. When IDs begin to meet other individual board members *outside* of the board setting in order to discuss matters to do with the organisation, this may be an indicator that that a board breakdown is afoot. Splitting off into different groups may indicate that the board is not functioning well at all. IDs should generally meet all together, or if that is not possible, circulate the minutes of their meetings with other IDs to those who were not present. This is not about suppressing discussion and/or dissent, both of which are crucial for a healthy board, but about maintaining trust and cooperation among *everyone*.

Any evidence of growing disquiet within the boardroom itself is a danger signal too. This is where different members will begin to either subtly, or not so subtly, manipulate others to come over to their way of thinking. This politicking is often fuelled by one particular individual who believes their position is under threat, or it may simply be a blatant power grab. Either way, it is not good for the smooth-running of the board.

Something all boards should be wary of is complete intransigence. Here, healthy debate about new strategies or directions are shut down with a 'That's not the way we do things around here' type of response. This resistance to change is entirely contrary to the boardroom ethos. Similarly, any sort of shared information bias should set off alarm bells. This is where the majority of board members stick doggedly with the information that is already known and which has been previously shared with the group. This resistance to reviewing any further evidence is hugely worrying.

How do boards come to a situation like this, where what seemed like a smooth-running organisation descends into something quite different? According to Jay Lorsch, the author of *Future of Boards: Meeting Governance Challenges of the Twenty-First Century*,[1] breakdowns in boardroom relationships often stem from underlying, yet unacknowledged, tensions. There may, for example, have been too much dissent during meetings, which was not properly managed by the chair. After a while, everyone will become exhausted and frustrated by the ensuing infighting and chaos which characterises each meeting. In a similar vein, there may be simply too much diversity of thought. While diversity is a good thing – indeed, I have spent much of this book arguing for its merits – it has to be properly managed. Diversity can't get in the way of good decision-making. There has to be a mechanism for reconciling differing viewpoints and working smoothly towards a rational consensus.

One thing many boards need to be wary of is giving disproportionate weight to the loudest voices in the room. It's easily done and most groups do usually defer to the most vocal and domineering member. However, this is very unhealthy in a boardroom setting where everyone has been brought in on the strength of their unique skills. Each person needs to be given the space to contribute and should be encouraged to do so. Even with careful management, this is not always easy, particularly for some of the executive directors. Their views might clash with the CEO, which means that it will take courage to speak. The CEO will also need to supress their ego to a certain degree too.

It is inevitable that not everything will pan out the way you expect. There may be unexpected problems or a significant disagreement. It is crucial to manage your reaction and to remain objective. Don't become emotional and certainly don't lecture your fellow board members. Equally importantly, don't avoid any issues – confront them directly. This is what you are there to do.

Of course, not all issues within boards have to be indicators of a looming meltdown. Something that may not be seen as quite as serious (at least not in the immediate timescale) is the issue of an inefficient board. What, then, does an ID do when they discover that what they believed to be a thriving, forward-thinking organisation actually turns out to be woefully badly run? The most obvious manifestations of this are meetings that always overrun as they repeatedly go over the same old ground with no decisions taken. In short, there is no sense of purpose and it is going nowhere.

In some circumstances, you will have to take the good with the bad and do the best with the hand you are dealt. It's a bit of a cliché to say the NHS is plodding and bureaucratic, and therefore a difficult environment in which to get anything done, but the IDs I spoke to all agreed that there were many frustrating elements to working for NHS Trusts. However, they found sides to it that were hugely rewarding too.

Dipti Amin, who began her portfolio ID career with a role on the Buckinghamshire NHS Trust, explains that she began with the understanding that it was a unique environment.

'Over the course of the first year, I visited many departments to see what they were doing at ground level. I spent a few hours with the spinal injuries unit, a half day with the cardiology team, and visited wards. There was the dual purpose of educating myself about the trust and meeting with staff saw, so I was not just this face on the website. It was a hugely valuable experience and gave me a much better understanding of what was happening. I saw all the challenges and a lot of people busting a gut. Yet, despite their efforts, it can be difficult to get things done.'

'The challenge is, where the financials are concerned, things like estate management and many of those sorts of structures are looked after centrally. They are partly out of the trust's control, especially if you are a non-foundation trust. This was difficult for someone like me, with a business background, who could see things from another perspective. I could see how we could do things more efficiently, yet the system limits what you can do. It can be frustrating at times.'

'Some people say, "I'm not sticking around for this rubbish," and leave. I totally understand how they feel, but I am also a bit disappointed because that's the easy thing to do. My view is that it's too important. It's better to hang in there and change things slowly. And, it will be slow. You are not trying to change the trust –

you are trying to influence change on a nationwide system. That means getting involved outside the committees and making sure we do the best job that we can. I'm quite hard to get rid of!'

Persistence and tenacity are key, when it comes to trying to change things from within. Clearly, as with Dipti's case, there needs to be a full understanding of the wider environment, but if there are opportunities for improvement, it is well worth raising any concerns with the chair. If board meetings begin to feel unfocussed and never seem to get to the point, consider having a quiet word. This is something that should also occur during the board appraisal process, but with many boards only conducting the appraisals every three years, and some not doing it at all, it may be prudent to raise any real concerns earlier. Board meetings do, after all, constitute the single most important part of an ID's contribution. It might simply be a case of focusing on the agenda of each board meeting, to see if this is the root cause of the problem. Perhaps the agenda is too geared towards reviewing past performance or catching up on external events. The anecdotes are interesting to hear, but are not necessarily helpful in moving things forward. There may even be a need to go back to basics and make sure that everyone is fully prepared and briefed for what lies ahead. Thus, when board papers are sent out, there should be a habit of everyone requesting any relevant background *before* the meeting, rather than interrupting strategic discussions to ask questions. Also, policy questions can be submitted ahead of meetings and then the chair can decide what to answer in advance so that precious meeting time is not consumed.

Another potential barrier to getting things done is that there has been too little time to socialise. Bear with me on this one. By this, I mean that the board has not earmarked space in the diary for board dinners or breakfasts, which means when the team does get together, too much of the agenda is hijacked as the team gets up to speed with one another. These informal relationships are crucial to the smooth-running of boards and need to be given time to flourish. They really do enhance a board's effectiveness, particularly in times of crises.

Being an ID does not come with any guarantees of an easy ride from boardroom colleagues. There are still occasionally situations where some board members are not always willing to give everyone a fair hearing, particularly on some voluntary boards which may not be nearly as well-regulated as corporate ones. It is not as common as it was, but it can still happen. Dissent can come in many forms too, from simply ignoring contributions from certain members, to less-than-subtle eye-rolling when someone speaks up and says something that is not 100% in alignment with their board colleagues. As a new ID, there is little choice in a situation like this but to persevere and work to change things from within. Often though, at least one of the other IDs will jump in and offer their support.

It should also be said that, now and again, board members can alienate their colleagues completely unintentionally. While we are (at last) entering an environment where diverse boards are gaining traction, not everyone is quite as enlightened as they might be. Mistakes are occasionally made as well-meaning board members do their best to accommodate new faces.

Jane Chafer, an ID at Plymouth Argyle, has an interesting example.

'An HR issue came up at my very first board meeting, involving a man sending crude pictures to his girlfriend. The board talked around the subject for some time, using this quasi-medical terminology, but to be honest they were so vague, I really didn't have a clue what they were saying. Eventually, I had to say something.'

'I said, *"You didn't sack this guy, but I am really not sure what he has done. You are talking to me in code. I don't know whether our response is proportionate or not."* There was a moment's silence before the chair explained the explicit nature of the photos in question. I thanked them for clearing it up and we moved on. It's just very funny now. We discuss things like normal people, just as everyone else does in real life.'

Jokes and well-meant misunderstandings aside, any boardroom scenario can be damaging when taken to the extreme. The thing is, though, all boards inevitably suffer from some conflict to one degree or another; it's part of the debating process. Both executives and IDs need to be aware of this and manage it as best they can. If any worrying signs emerge, such as increased factionist behaviour, then everyone needs to be prepared to act. Strong leadership is, of course, crucial when it comes to preventing the boardroom spiralling into any of these scenarios, but so also is the continued enthusiasm and participation of the IDs.

Note

1 Jay Lorsch, *Future of Boards: Meeting Governance Challenges of the Twenty-First Century*, Harvard Business Review Press, July 2012.

Chapter 11
Finding your voice and growing your role

It's extremely important to realise, and to go on realising, that the people running things don't necessarily always know it all. IDs have to be prepared to understand and then question why things are happening. Otherwise, there'll be a situation where the board believes it is supporting management to the ends of the earth, but in reality, they will be supporting them down the drain.

Sarah Turvill, Chair of Council, University of Exeter

In the past, there have been three categories of IDs, which I have dubbed the Good, the Bad and the Ugly. The Good develop into useful IDs, thanks to their independent nature, integrity and professional attitude. The Bad are the ones who sadly go native. Despite early good intentions, they prove to be poor communicators, have low attention levels and slip into the unhelpful approach of trying to do the executive job. Worst of all, though, are the Ugly, who are irresponsible, corrupt and consumed by their self-interests.

As we have seen throughout the book, the stakes are high. There have been a succession of issues arising from chronic mismanagement, and this is your opportunity to help address this imbalance. As an ID, you can make a difference and help create a new vision for not just the organisation that you align yourself with, but also contribute to the sector as a whole. This is your opportunity to apply a unique perspective and really make a difference.

IDs should recognise that the role is constantly developing. It is not simply a case of securing a position, or a handful of positions, and then sitting back for the ride. Far from it. The role is evolving in every sector, in line with changes in the wider environment. Boards need to be constantly looking ahead and making sure that their IDs are well-versed in the required skills and regulations in order to drive their best performance and continue to make a difference. Naturally, IDs play a crucial role in this endeavour.

Continuous development is becoming more important than ever in modern boards. There is, quite rightly, an increasing focus on ensuring that IDs have a broad range of skills, including being strong on finance. This is the way to ensure complete transparency. If everyone understands every aspect of the way an organisation is being run, there will be vastly less potential for surprises later on. Similarly, there is a need for a full and up-to-date understanding of regulatory, legal, accountancy and tax rules, all of which are constantly changing.

As a young director coming up through the ranks, I have occasionally found the issue of board appraisals and director development an awkward and uncomfortable conversation. There still exists an old-school view that you are either qualified and have the experience to be on a board, or not. This was quite an eye-opener for me, because I feel strongly that everyone always has

https://doi.org/10.1515/9783110706123-011

some development needs. I am lucky to have had the support of two excellent chairs, Norman Gascoigne (Warwickshire County Cricket Club) and Andy Reed OBE (Sports and Play Construction Association, SAPCA), who both understand the importance of staying ahead of the curve. I am very grateful to them for encouraging my development as a director.

I recently completed my FT NED Director Exams. Why? Because I wanted to be the best board director that I could possibly be. One of the FT modules was about behaviour and I learned a huge amount here. It gave me an understanding about the often-mistaken assumptions we make about how we are relating to others on the board. It's really powerful to have some insight to that, and obviously it is something that feeds back into the job we do on the board. It's hugely valuable.

This education has given me access to best practices and the latest thinking to underpin my promotion to the senior independent director (SID) role at Warwickshire, so that I continue to develop and add value to the board.

I'd like to see more people putting themselves out there to improve themselves.

Michelle Leavesley, ID Warwickshire CCC, Sport & Play Construction Association, British Wheelchair Basketball

There are a number of training courses on offer to assist experienced IDs. The goal is to make them aware of board issues and help them respond to challenges, as well as introduce or develop skills, which may enhance their role.

IDs in public companies are subject to performance appraisals, which is another requirement of the corporate governance code, as recommended by the Higgs Review, of 2003. These appraisals are part of the board evaluations discussed at the end of Chapter 6. They should be seen as a valuable part of director development, rather than a mild inconvenience. The goal of the appraisal is to confirm that the board does still have a suitable balance of skills among all its members, who each have a good range of knowledge and understanding.

Board effectiveness is not simply down to the skills and experiences of individuals. As we saw in the previous chapter, some boards fail to function well because of interpersonal dynamics, such as personality clashes, or one or two overbearing members dictating the direction of travel. However, regular assessments are an incredibly useful starting point to identifying imbalances, both on an individual skills basis and on a wider scale. IDs should certainly use the opportunity of appraisals to assist in identifying any gaps in their skills or knowledge, and to suggest ways to improve via further training.

Aside from keeping up their personal development, there is another important onus placed upon all IDs. It is crucial that they remain refreshed and focused on the task on hand, even after a few years in the post when the initial enthusiasm may have worn off. It's not always an easy thing to do, particularly if the environment is challenging and you have not been able to achieve as much as you would have liked. However, if you are not fully switched on, it will affect your decision-making, productivity and creative thinking.

IDs need to make sure they retain their energy and inquisitiveness. This means reading board papers just as diligently as they did on the first day, even after a few years in post. If they find that they are beginning to skip over this a little, it is a warning sign that needs to be addressed. Similarly, they should be just as active within the boardroom, asking relevant questions and actively participating. However, there should be an active effort to keep contributions fresh. You don't want to become known as the person on the board who is always banging on about the same old thing. While there may be a subject or area that you feel strongly about, if you begin to sound like a broken record, your board colleagues will almost certainly tune out after a while, even if the point is quite valid and worth pursuing. You don't have to drop the subject completely. Simply find a way to make the point differently, or offer it in an alternative way, to guard against over-familiarity. IDs should also keep well-informed about developments in the sector and devote sufficient time to site visits.

A key part of maintaining the energy and enthusiasm is to be constantly on the look-out for ways to improve things. There has been much discussion in this book about increased moves to encouraging diversity on boards and I strongly believe that every ID should consciously be a strong advocate in this respect. Everyone has a role to play in looking at their own boards and wondering if there is anything they can do to encourage and accommodate a more diverse base. Paralympian Liz Johnson told me about just one such simple adjustment that made it easier for IDs on Disability Sport Wales.

'I noticed that we always held board meetings at the same time of the day, on the same day of the week, every time we had one,' she said. 'We realised that this was not entirely beneficial for all of the attendees and that the same people were forever having to rearrange things to be at the meeting. This was not in anyone's interests, particularly since you want as many people as possible to attend each meeting and we wanted a diverse range of new recruits. We needed to be more flexible.'

'There is a lot of potential for more sports and voluntary boards to do this. They can vary the meetings days and times or, even better, run the meetings out of work time. This sort of flexibility will inevitably attract a wider range of people to the board.'

'Diversification is a strength. If you want positive change, and you want your voluntary organisation or sports governing body, or whatever it is, to best serve its community, then you need to think carefully about what you are offering appointees and how you work with them.'

As an ID role develops, some IDs may become concerned that the calls on their time seem to become ever more onerous. There might seem like an increasing number of regulatory and compliance issues to get to grips with, and audit and accounting demands may appear increasingly complex. That's not to mention the never-ending developments in technology that IDs need to keep abreast of so that they can assess, quantify and advise the board on what is relevant. Meanwhile, there are demands for input around key issues regarding organisational strategy and operations, where senior management need advice and wise guidance in an increasingly competitive environment. IDs who are members of board committees will also need to allocate extra time to these activities.

There is no doubt that time management is a key issue for IDs, particularly for those who are managing their duties alongside a full-time role elsewhere. While most companies are highly supportive of their executives taking up ID roles, since it is useful for their personal development, there is a balance to be had. If too much time is spent out of the office or perusing board papers, questions will begin to be asked. The important thing is to be considerate to your main employer and remind yourself why you took on ID roles in the first place.

> I did often find myself out of the office and travelling a huge amount. It was always important to me to be there for board meetings and I think I only missed one in nine years. It can be really difficult sometimes. There used to be occasions when I'd do a board meeting at Leap in the early evening and then go to the airport to get out to Singapore. Or, I'd arrive back from the US and go straight to a board meeting. If you've got a serious corporate role as well, it is exciting, but also logistically challenging.
>
> Occasionally, while I was still at 3i, somebody would say, 'How come you do this? You really should be totally dedicated to the corporate.' My response was, 'Actually, I think I give more, because I learned a lot from those other ventures.' I think it grounds you in a way that's helpful, and absolutely forces you to prioritize your time.
>
> I was in South Africa one time, standing in the middle of a slum, which was a forbidding place. I had this call from a colleague. We'd just refreshed the corporate identity and introduced a whole new range of business cards. He was ringing me up to complain about how his business cards looked. I was at that very moment sitting with a community worker and young girl who was a survivor of sexual violence that day and was frightened to go to school. So, I said to him, 'I'm really sorry, but I've got a choice to make, and that's whether I'm going to have this conversation now, or have it next week, or indeed whether we have it at all. Let me just tell you what I'm doing.'
>
> It was cruel on the guy, but I think he got the picture. He said, 'Oh, not at all, not at all. It doesn't really matter at all.' And it didn't. It was not something to get excited about, even in the corporate sector. The best thing is that that episode gave us both a sense of priority. In corporate life, you do spend a lot of time worrying about stuff that doesn't really make any difference at all.
>
> I've found that the charity roles have helped me over the years. Apart from the incredible fulfilment, it's really helped me understand what matters commercially, as well as in the social sector sense, too.
>
> **Patrick Dunne, ID roles include Boardelta, EY Foundation, ESSA and Leap**

Even when roles are fulfilling, time management is a crucial part of running ID roles alongside a full-time career elsewhere. Indeed, it should also be a key factor when you are running a plural career, since no one wants to waste their own time, or the time of their colleagues on a board. IDs should guard against being too *reactive* in their roles, which can put pressure on an already stretched time resource. In other words, it is not uncommon for IDs to put responsibility for time management onto the chair, allowing them to dictate which activities require an ID's presence and when. While, as we have seen here, the chairman does indeed play a crucial role in the conduct of the board and its meetings, and is naturally more on top of the critical issues facing an organisation, board effectiveness is the responsibility for every individual director. It is therefore up to each ID to be proactive about how they and the board spend their time and what activities they are able to participate in. This will involve clearly identifying areas to focus on, planning for and setting aside sufficient time for key activities and ensuring that essential activities are prioritised. It's in everyone's best interest to use time efficiently.

At the other end of the scale, there are also time-sapping activities that IDs should most certainly avoid. IDs should always be wary about crossing the invisible line and expending more and more time advising the CEO and other executives on the details, or trying to micromanage strategy. This is not the role of an ID. Board members must always remain vigilant about their responsibilities and the areas of expertise that they bring to the board.

If you do find that you are no longer contributing in the way that you would like, or feel that you have come to the end of the road, it may be time to move on. The 2018 UK Corporate Governance Code recommends no more than a nine-year tenure for IDs, because after this point it believes they can no longer be assumed to be independent. Corporate governance experts are, however, usually tolerant of one or two long-serving directors who were classed as independent when they first joined a board, but clusters of IDs who have been around for more than nine years should ring alarm bells. None of this means that every ID has to hang on for the full nine years. It is not uncommon for IDs to change position after three. Things are often more flexible in boards that operate outside the strict realms of a corporate setting.

Moving on to pastures new, or new ID positions, does not mean an immediate and final parting of ways. Many of the IDs interviewed for this book spoke about assisting their boards to identify and recruit their successor. They are well-placed to do so, too, since they understand the role and its requirements and may well have connections who have similar skills. Likewise, there may also be a need to mentor successors in order to affect a seamless transition. If an ID helps to reduce any steep learning curve that they may have had, it opens the way for the next in line to help move an organisation on even further.

The good news is that once you have completed a term like this, finding a fresh ID position will not be anywhere as challenging as it was when you first started out on this path. In fact, it is quite likely that organisations will approach *you* with offers. Certainly, this will be the case if you have maintained your profile and kept up with your networking, as detailed earlier. Again, though, there is no compulsion to take the first options offered. Stick to the tried and tested path and do careful due diligence with each new position.

Afterword

There are not many people who did not spend at least part of the coronavirus lockdown imagining what the new normal would look like. For some, this thinking confirmed the fact that they should enjoy what they have a little more and take time to value their family and close friends. Perhaps, too, they vowed to spend less money on stuff they didn't really need and take a step back to enjoy what they already have. For others, their thoughts turned to wider aspects of life: How can they use this terrible shock to the global order to help make the world a better place in the future?

There is much to be said for viewing the 'What next?' question in a wider sense. The pandemic amplified many times over what is wrong in society and, quite rightly, opened up watershed conversations about the need for deep social, political and economic change. Much of the focus has been on hospitals and care homes, but it is clear that the malaise goes far deeper and that all sections of society are at a crossroads. There needs to be some drastic and long-lasting changes. We have already seen some promising signs that the conversation has begun. Independent public heath campaigners such as Medact and Every Doctor have focussed attention on the real needs of the NHS, while the Institute of Public Policy Research thinktank has been a powerful voice in arguing that bailouts for companies should necessitate action on their social responsibilities and work towards a more moral economy. Meanwhile, Green New Deal UK's Build Back Better has lobbied hard for a new political settlement that 'prioritises people, invests in our NHS and creates a robust, shockproof economy that is capable of tackling climate crisis'. At the time of writing, there are plenty of other campaign groups gearing up to make sure that those thoughts we all had during the pandemic are translated into positive momentum towards improvements in society. It is not something that can simply be left to others, though. We all have a responsibility to get involved now and, as I have outlined in this book, I believe that one of the best ways to contribute is by becoming an independent director. This is the way to push for change from within and to make sure that the way the wider world responds to the aftermath of the health crisis is in everyone's interest. It can't just be business as usual.

Stepping up to become an ID is not the easy option. We now live in a very different world than the one before Covid-19. Everyone and everything have been profoundly affected by the health crisis. We are now in a recession, thousands of businesses have gone to the wall, public services are stretched to the limit and untold numbers of individual households have seen their financial prospects reduced to tatters. Whichever organisation you choose to join as an ID will be facing some big questions about its future. While the health service has achieved a new level of affection and gratitude in the hearts of the population, it is still chronically underfunded. The same goes for social care, which bore so much of the brunt of the

https://doi.org/10.1515/9783110706123-012

pandemic. Charities have seen many of their numbers close, and those that are left are having to drastically rethink, with donations cut to the bone. Universities, a sector I know well, are facing an unprecedented funding crisis without the certainty of fees from international students. This is on top of an already fragile model for so many educational institutions. Meanwhile, there are so many clubs, community centres and sporting organisations that are wondering how much longer they can survive at a time when these places are so vital to rebuilding communities that were shuttered for so long. Plus, there is still a need to make sure that groups advocating for more awareness over everything from climate change to gender equality and animal rights, have their voices heard among all the noise of those trying to rebuild and reach the new normal.

An ID role, or similar equivalent role, will open up a wide range of opportunities to improve things from the inside and have a real, noticeable impact. With perseverance and dedication, it is possible to make a meaningful contribution to changing the direction of travel and ensure that causes and institutions close to your heart are given the right attention and momentum to achieve what they have been set up to achieve. Equally important, you will be able to play a crucial role in stopping boardroom abuses and inefficiencies in their tracks – issues which can and do adversely affect a huge range of people, often in devastating ways.

Everyone's starting point will vary. For some, this will be an opportunity to get back into the workplace, learn new skills and, perhaps, find an entirely new and more satisfying direction. Others will be adding this activity to their day jobs. All being well, we will see an increase in interest to take up the offer of employer-supported volunteering (ESV) schemes that offer employees paid time off to volunteer during working hours. At present, just 16% of ESV volunteers are becoming trustees, or members of committees. There is clearly room for many, many more people to take up the opportunity. The structure is in place – all you need to do is step forward and take advantage of it.

My starting point for writing this book was motivated by my passionate belief that we need a wider range of people to step up and make a difference. Studies after studies have shown the value of diverse boards, and those boards that have listened to this advice have reaped the benefits, as have the stakeholders of those organisations they represent. It won't happen overnight – indeed, right now it all feels like a long, slow haul – but the only way to make progress is if people step forward.

We also need organisations to match this enthusiasm and momentum and to embrace the undoubted opportunities that a wider pool of skills and opinions represent. There needs to be a shift in opinion and outlook, but that is never a bad thing, particularly right now. Even little steps in this direction, such as varying the time and place of board meetings, can make things easier for young people who need to negotiate time away from the day job if there are no ESV capabilities, and those who are juggling the needs of bringing up children. Chairs have a key role to play here, supporting individuals who are learning their skills on the job and helping them to find their voice. Again, it is to everyone's advantage.

I have not shied away from outlining some of the challenges involved in seeking out and taking up ID positions. Not all boards are prepared for change and, of those that are, often there are many outside influences and regulations that make the pace of change appear painfully slow. There is a lot to do too. Certainly, the responsibilities of governance and accountability are far, far more onerous than they were ten years ago. Plus, now there is far less money around, there is constant pressure to find new, innovative and legitimate ways of keeping organisations solvent, profitable and fulfilling their purpose. On a purely logistical level, there will be a certain amount of time juggling involved, particularly if the ID is already in a full-time role. He or she will also have to make sure their boss is fully on board with their aspirations and manage their calendar carefully so that no one is at a disadvantage.

The benefits of stepping up run both ways. As well as having a hugely positive impact on the organisations that are being offered the service of a greater range of eminently qualified IDs, there is a lot of enjoyment and satisfaction to be had from serving on boards. All of the IDs I spoke to voiced the tremendous personal fulfilment derived from becoming an ID. They also felt the experience improved their knowledge and personal development, which in turn was beneficial in their day-to-day roles. In some cases, it might open up an entirely new and welcome direction in your career. Becoming an ID is a great way to realise skills and interests you may not have previously known about.

Landing that first ID role will be a challenge. It won't happen overnight and will require an active strategy of networking and putting yourself in front of the right people to find what you are looking for. Nevertheless, any ID is advised to think carefully about the roles they will accept and should certainly do extensive due diligence during the interview stage. Not only will this stand you in good stead for the application, but it will also help you determine whether you really will be able to make a tangible difference, which is, after all, the point.

If you find a role that you feel passionate about, and you get to the interview stage, prepare well. Consider why the board should choose *you*. What is it that you will be bringing to the boardroom? What is it in your background and experiences that will be particularly valuable to the board?

The skills and qualities that individual organisations are looking for will vary from organisation to organisation, but there are certain generic qualities that will always stand out and be highly regarded. When recruiting IDs, the values of the potential candidates are key. Whether it is for a role in the health service, or a charity, or a sports club, organisations will want to be reassured that the people coming forward have the right motivations and want the best for that sector. They don't want someone who is just along for the ride. In terms of specifics, listening skills are key. Anyone who just wants to talk, or is all about transmitting but not receiving, is not suitable. Active participation is another valued skill, because it indicates commitment and reliability. Boards need IDs that turn up regularly, having read the papers and reflected upon them. An open mind and readiness to learn is key, too. Communication is important, and IDs should be capable of encouraging and persuading, which are key skills when it comes to making views known and opening up a new way of considering or tackling problems. IDs will never have total control – they need to find a different way to make things happen. They should also be prepared to ask *a lot* of questions.

If any organisation is going to recover from recent global events and rebuild itself for the future, it needs a wide range of skills around its boardroom table. There is an increased demand for experts in disciplines such as digital and international business. There is also more importance placed on *every* ID being financially literate. Prospective IDs should think carefully about what skills they have to offer.

Once you do get that role, there should ideally be a formal induction programme so you can hit the ground running. If this is not the case, you will need to create one of your own. Ask to visit the organisation and meet with as many key senior people as you can. Research its background and that of the rest of the sector, and familiarise yourself with all of the relevant issues that might be discussed in the boardroom. If you do your homework well, you will be less inhibited when it comes to asking the really crucial questions. Remember also that what might initially sound like a really stupid enquiry often turns out to be truly insightful.

After joining a board, have the courage to actively contribute and work at building relationships with your fellow board members. Ask the chair how you are getting on and listen to the feedback. It is only by doing all of these things that you will make progress. Above all, remember that you are there to support the management right up until the time when you can't support them. Your ultimate sanction, which can only be used once, is to remove the chief executive. If you are not prepared to do this, you will never be able to fully execute your responsibilities.

In my view, we are standing on the threshold of a new opportunity, which can easily transform the way so many of our nation's best-known and lesser-known organisations are run, at a time when they most need our help. We know that diversification can bring great strengths to the boardroom and now more than ever, we need every advantage that we can find. The only way to make it happen is if more people take ID roles. As I hope this book has shown, the arguments in favour of broader representation in the boardroom are as strong as ever. It is not just effective in guarding against future scandals but also in helping organisations work in a far more focused and efficient way, which is of course to everyone's advantage. It won't happen by accident. Both sides of the divide have a part to play. Organisations need to make diversity an active part of their recruitment strategy at all levels, including the boardroom, and people from all walks of life need to step forward and be prepared to make their mark.

While there is a finite number of corporate ID roles, there are enormous numbers of charity, social and voluntary boardroom positions on offer. Similarly, there are numerous pressure groups that are crying out for the help of qualified, talented people. Many are really struggling to make an impact and your involvement could transform their outlook. For many people, this will be exactly the challenge they are looking for to give something back to society. For others, these smaller roles are a great stepping stone to building up an ID career with multiple appointments. Whatever your motivations, it is to the advantage of everyone if more people opt to become IDs.

If you want to make a difference, the first step is to commit to becoming an ID.

List of interviewees

Dipti Amin

Dr. Dipti Amin is currently director at Maaya Associates, Ltd. and a non-executive director on the Boards of Buckinghamshire Healthcare NHS Trust, Cambridge Innovation Capital and the University of Hertfordshire. Previously, she was chief compliance officer at Quintiles Transnational (now Iqvia), and over the last 27 years Dr. Amin has held positions of operational and strategic responsibility within pharmaceutical services at the C-suite and board level. Her broad experience covers clinical pharmacology, ethical issues in clinical research, drug development, ethics and compliance programmes as well as leadership and management of large, multi-functional, multi-geographical, global groups to deliver value-added, efficient growth and achieving business turnarounds. Dr. Amin is an honorary lecturer in clinical pharmacology at Guy's, King's, and St. Thomas' Hospitals Medical & Dental Schools. Previously, Dr. Amin served on the Board of the Faculty of Pharmaceutical Medicine of the Royal College of Physicians, on the Innovation Board and Medical Expert Network of the Association of the British Pharmaceutical Industry, on a Department of Health Multi-centre Research Ethics Committee, on the Emerging Science and Bioethics Advisory Committee of the Dept. of Health, and on the Board of Governors of Heathfield School for Girls (The Girls' Day School Trust).

Richard Atkins

Richard Atkins was appointed further Education Commissioner in October 2016. He was previously a college principal for 21 years, initially at Yeovil College and then at Exeter College. During his tenure at Exeter, the college was judged outstanding by Ofsted and won several national awards for excellence. Richard has spent over 35 years working in FE colleges as a teacher and leader and has held a number of national positions, including president of the Association of Colleges and a commissioner for adult and vocational learning. Richard is also a pro chancellor and member of council at the University of Exeter.

Helen Baker

Helen Baker has held board-level executive and non-executive leadership roles in the not-for-profit and public sectors across a career spanning health, social care, housing and education. She brings particular skills in the fields of mental health and disability, in public policy and in the governance and regulation of public services.

Helen has chaired organisations ranging from NHS trusts to national housing associations and social care providers, a multi-academy trust and both local and national charities. She has held board appointments with three government arms-length bodies: the General Social Care Council, the Commission for the Compact and the National College for School Leadership.

She is currently the Chair of Shelter and on the board of the What Works Centre for Wellbeing. She continues as a trustee of the Association of Chairs, the national body supporting the work of charity chairs and is also a Deputy Lieutenant for Oxfordshire.

Ruth Cairnie

Ruth Cairnie has recently been appointed chair at Babcock International Group PLC. She is also a non-executive director at Rolls-Royce Holdings and Associated British Foods PLC. She is the SID at ABF and chairs the Remuneration Committees at Rolls-Royce and ABF. She was previously on the boards of Keller Group plc and ContourGlobal PLC. She sits on the finance committee of Cambridge University and chairs the POWERful Women initiative. She is a trustee of Windsor Leadership.

Ruth left Royal Dutch Shell in 2014 after a 37-year career spanning research, B2B businesses, strategy, supply chain and M&A. Her roles included EVP for Strategy and Planning,

https://doi.org/10.1515/9783110706123-013

responsible for the development of global Group strategy, and chief executive of Shell's global Commercial Fuels business.

Ruth has a BSc Joint Honours in Mathematics & Physics from Bristol University, a Masters in Advanced Studies from Cambridge University and she undertook the Corporate Finance programme at London Business School.

Jane Chafer

Jane Chafer has had a marketing and communications career that has taken her from mining to chocolate to telecoms and higher education. She has held senior positions at both Sheffield and Plymouth before joining the executive team at the University of Exeter as the Director of Communications and Corporate Affairs in February 2014. A Chartered Marketer and fellow of the Charted Institute of Marketing, Jane held the position of Chair for the Universities Marketing Forum, before handing over the baton in August 2019. In addition to being a member of the Vice-Chancellor's Executive Group at Exeter, Jane also sit on the boards of Falmouth Exeter Plus and INTO Exeter. Jane is also a member of the Falmouth Exeter Plus Board, joining colleagues from both University of Exeter and Falmouth University. Another interest for Jane is Plymouth Argyle Football Club where she is a non-executive director. Jane regularly attends matches to cheer on the 'Green Army'!

Jane started her career in 1985 with a marketing sponsorship for ECC Limited, based in St. Austell, and completed a BSc in Business Studies at Bradford University, with a six-month spell in Milan. This was followed by a move to Mars confectionery and subsequently BT, where she held various senior marketing and communication roles with responsibility for integrated customer-facing campaigns and communications. In 2009 Jane, completed an MBA at Ashridge.

Mike Clancy

Mike Clancy is the owner of recruitment services firm Walgrove. He founded the company in 2009 and focuses on board appointments (Chair, NED and CEO) for UK SME's. In 2015, international recruitment capability was added via membership of the Cornerstone International Network and in 2018, a career transition service for executives looking to start the non-executive phase of their career was launched. Since 2016 he has been a speaker on the FT NED Diploma course and is an ambassador for both Nurole, the online board level hiring platform, and Women on Boards, a support network focused on helping the next generation of female directors. Mike has been involved in the recruitment of non-executive directors since 2001 when he led a team at a mid-sized recruitment firm assisting private equity clients to appoint independent chairmen and non-executive directors to the boards of their investee companies. In his early career, he worked at a quoted investment business and consumer conglomerate, Grand Metropolitan PLC (now Diageo PLC). He is a graduate of the London Business School MBA programme and an Economic History graduate from the University of Edinburgh.

Patrick Dunne

Patrick Dunne is chair of board consultancy Boardelta, the charities the EY Foundation and Education Sub Saharan Africa (ESSA) and a trustee of the Chartered Management Institute. He has extensive experience of developing social enterprises, most notably with Leap Confronting Conflict where he is patron and was chairman, from 2006 to 2015, with ESSA, the EY Foundation and with Warwick in Africa, which he founded in 2006. Warwick in Africa has now benefited over 700,000 young Africans with transformed maths and English teaching.

His executive career was in the chemicals and private equity sectors with Air Products and 3i Group plc where, until 2012, he was communications director, a member of its Operating committee and chairman of its Operational Risk forum.

Patrick is the author of three successful books on 'boards', including *Boards*, which won in the HR and Management category in the 2020 Business Book of the Year awards. He is a member of the Higgs Review and also a visiting professor at Cranfield School of Management, associate fellow at Warwick Business School and a former member of the General Council of the University of Warwick.

Janie Frampton

Janie Frampton has been an active football referee for 29 years and became the second woman to have operated within men's professional football. She worked at the FA for 12 years as National Referee Manager for Education and Training, delivering education to grassroots through to elite referees on every continent and within every confederation on behalf of The FA and FIFA. As one of eight female FIFA Instructors in the world, she has been privileged to be involved in many FIFA World Cups and workshops.

Janie is a founding Trustee of Ref Support UK Charity and honorary CEO for Sports Officials UK, Ltd., an umbrella organisation for the education and development of sports officials across all sports. She has been voted in as vice president of the new World Organisation for sports officials; International Federation for Sports Officials which is based in the Hague

Other appointments include being an independent director for the English Cricket Board for four years, patron for the Muslim Women's Network UK, National Ambassador for Women in Football, Vice Chair of Boccia England and Executive Chair of the International Socca Federation (the world governing body for small sided football). Janie is also director of her own Sports Officials Consultancy for sports officials working across all sports in the education and development of sports officials

Jonathan Hurst

Jonathan is a non-executive director and chair of audit committee at two family-owned businesses, one of which owns and operates holiday and residential parks in the UK, and the other manufactures duvets and pillows in the UK, Europe and Australia. He is also an independent director at a UK headquartered international legal firm. Prior to becoming an independent director, Jonathan was a partner at KPMG, sitting on the UK Board and ran their Northern region, covering offices in Manchester, Leeds, Newcastle, Liverpool and Preston. He was an audit partner specialising in the retail and consumer goods sector, with a client base ranging from large private businesses to listed companies. Jonathan is an avid Manchester United supporter, loves all sport and stays fit exercising his two-year old cockapoo, Tedster.

Liz Johnson

Liz Johnson started swimming at the age of 3, following advice that it would help with her cerebral palsy. By the age of 14, she was already competing at a national level and made the British team shortly after. Liz won Gold at the 2008 and 2012 Paralympics, as well as a clutch of World Championship medals. In addition to her swimming successes, Liz graduated as an accountant in 2008 with a degree in business management and finance. Since retiring from the pool, she became the co-founder of the Ability People, an employment agency staffed exclusively by people with impairments. She is also on the board of Disability Sport Wales.

Michelle Leavesley

Michelle Leavesley is an experienced executive and non-executive having held several senior roles in risk management brand and marketing communications and has been a female pioneer on sports boards. She is currently director of organisational risk & resilience at M&G PLC. Prior to this she established a highly successful brand and marketing communications agency which delivered several major social marketing campaigns, led the MSc Marketing Communications programme at Birmingham Business School and worked in international sports events and major infrastructure investment projects for the Lawn Tennis Association. Michelle's first non-executive appointment was in 2007 onto a Sport England Regional Board and she joined p British Wheelchair Basketball following the 2012 Olympic and Paralympic Games held in London. She was appointed to the board of Warwickshire County Cricket Club in 2014 and became the senior independent director in 2020. Michelle successfully passed the FT NED Diploma and loves golf.

Richard Sargeant

Richard Sargeant is the chief commercial officer at Faculty. He supports senior leaders across a variety of sectors to transform their organisations to make AI real. Before joining Faculty, he was a director of digital & data transformation at the Home Office and a founding director of the UK government's digital service. Before that, he worked at Google as their UK Head of Public Policy, which he joined after running the Gowers' Review of Intellectual Property, among other projects, while a senior policy advisor in HM Treasury. His first role in government was in the Prime Minister's Strategy Unit, writing papers on innovation in the public sector and happiness. He also co-founded Engineers Without Borders UK. He is a non-executive director on the board of the government's Centre for Data Ethics and Innovation and has had previous non-executive roles at Exeter University and the Challenge Network.

Sir Peter Thompson

Sir Peter Thompson spent much of his working life in the field of logistics, ending his career as chairman and chief executive of the National Freight Corporation. He led the team which bought the company from the government in a most successful employee buy-out. It was a great success and formed the raison d'être for the inclusion of an employee share offer in all the subsequent privatisations. Sir Peter Thompson was knighted and awarded Businessman of the Year in 1995 for his contribution to business management.

Since his retirement, Sir Peter Thompson has continued in the role of chairman and 'business angel' to many private companies in a diverse range of industries including green energy, land trading, medical analysis and theatre production companies.

Sarah Turvill

Sarah Turvill has been chair of council of the University of Exeter since 2012. She retired in December 2013 as chairperson of Willis International. Having joined Willis in 1978 to establish a legal department, she spent 14 years there dealing with general legal advice, managing the advice of external lawyers, acquisitions start-ups/disposals, and dealing with international operations. In 1991 when Willis needed to establish an international network of offices, Sarah led the negotiations and legal work. The following year, Sarah moved from the legal department to become the operations director of Continental Europe, before being appointed chief executive of Continental Europe in 1995. 2001 saw Sarah appointed chief executive of the International Operations of Willis and a member of the Group Executive Committee and in 2011 she was appointed as chairperson of Willis International. Sarah is an alumna of the University (LLB Hons 1975); she was called to the Bar in 1976 and appointed a Bencher at Gray's Inn in 2009.

Devyani Vaishampayan

Devyani Vaishampayan is the managing partner of the HR TECH Partnership, a People Tech Investment venture whose investors are all senior non-executive/corporate directors. Set up in London in 2016, the focus of the People TECH Fund is investment in Employee/Talent Digital

Technology start-ups. The HR TECH Partnership also runs Human Capital Digital Innovation Hubs, which help corporates/HR teams learn and experiment around the 'Future of Work'.

Prior to this, Devyani has been an international and multi-sector Group CHRO and board member effectively leading large, diverse and multi-billion complex organizations through transformational change. She has had global roles in successful organizations across various industries such as Citibank, AT&T, British Gas, Rolls Royce and Petronas. Having lived and worked in China, Singapore and Europe (and managed teams in the Americas & Middle East), she is very international in her outlook.

Devyani, who has been featured on the 2017 Financial Times Ethnic Minority Leaders List and 2016 FTSE 100 'Women to Watch', is considered a Thought Leader around the Future of Work and blends a unique perspective of digital innovation and investment along with the practical perspective of a practitioner.

Appendix

Resources

A. Characteristics of a good ID

Personal

Integrity
Judgement
Leadership
Motivation
Communication skills
Interpersonal sensitivity
Listening skills
Intelligence
Cultural flexibility
Sense of responsibility
Independence

Professional and managerial

Strategy
Technical
Organisational
Analytical
Problem solving
Chairing
Committee membership (audit, remuneration, nomination)

Entrepreneurial

Vision
Judgement
Conviction
Decisiveness
Commercial acumen

https://doi.org/10.1515/9783110706123-014

B. Board evaluation checklist will include the following

1. Overall impression of the board
   - Dynamics of the board
   - Culture and climate in the boardroom
   - Sense of teamwork
   - Quality of discussion/balance of debate
2. Organisation of the board
   - Agendas, formation of agendas and coverage of the right topics
   - Reporting, including of board committees
   - Meeting frequency and length
   - Formal processes and duties
   - Informal processes (including board dinners)
   - Strategy sessions
   - Information and support materials: company secretariat and support
3. Committee organisation: Audit, remuneration, health, safety & environment, nomination
   - Agendas
   - Meeting frequency and length
   - Membership, internal attendees and adviser attendees
   - Information and support materials
   - Topics for the board versus topics for the committees
4. Board composition
   - Size
   - Balance
   - Skill sets
   - Independence
   - Rotation
5. Board involvement and engagement
   - Directors' knowledge of the business
   - Relationships with management
   - Contact outside the boardroom
   - Strategy development
   - Induction and training for new directors
6. Communication with shareholders/stakeholders
   - Shareholder messages
   - Analyst meetings and reports
   - AGM
   - Chairman's role with shareholders/stakeholders
   - Other directors' role with shareholders/stakeholders

Looking forward

7. Looking forward
   - Succession planning (executive and independent)
   - Directors' development needs
8. Overall board effectiveness
   - Progress since last board evaluation
   - Fulfilment of fiduciary duties
   - Ethics, Corporate Social Responsibility and environment
   - Compliance with UK Corporate Governance Code
   - Expectations placed on directors including their responsibilities for governance and remuneration
   - Support to the business
   - Checks and balances
   - Short- and long-term health of the business
9. Colleagues
   - Chairman
   - Senior independent director
   - Chairmen
   - Independent directors
   - Executive directors

C. Search firms

aimsinternational.com
boyden.com
directorbank.com
draxexecutive.com
egonzehnder.com
forbeshr.com
harveynash.com
heidrick.com
kornferry.com
odgersberndtson.com
skillcapital.com
spectrum-ehcs.com
spencerstuart.com
tyzack.com

D. ID training courses

IoD – Role of Non-Executive Director

This one-day course outlines practical strategies from the point when you begin to build your network, to what to do when you first secure an appointment. Legal and practical responsibilities are covered, along with strategies to help new IDs to add value in the boardroom and deal with challenges. The courses are presented by experienced IDs and guest speakers who will also give tips on specifics, such as interview techniques. The session ends with a drinks reception and an opportunity to network.

Cost £1,310 (non-members)
https://www.iod.com/training/opencourses

Financial Times – Non-Executive Director Programme

The *Financial Times* runs a series of courses for IDs, from 'So you want to be a *Non-Executive Director*', a one-day course which covers the basic duties and liabilities, as well as advice on effective boardroom behaviour, to the *Effective Non-Executive Director Programme*, which is a two-day intensive course focussing on increasing an ID's contribution to a board. A series of board masterclasses hone in on specifics such as international board dynamics, the effective remuneration committee and appointing the right CEO.

Cost: from £375
https://Non-execs.ft.com/Financial-Times/NED

Henley Business School – Board Directors' Programme

The two-day residential programme aims to provide a 'toolbox of vital skills and leadership capabilities' to help attendees understand what being an ID truly entails. Topics covered include how to influence and manage dysfunctional boards, stakeholders' perspectives and engagement, mentoring and the importance of corporate, social and community responsibility.

Cost: £2,550
https://www.henley.ac.uk/executive-education/course/the-board-directors-programme

Pwc/Cass Business School – Professional Development Programme for Non-Executive Directors

The emphasis of this one-day course is on planning and preparing for a first appointment. As well as outlining the key players and responsibilities on the wider board, it hones in on individual roles, responsibilities, strategies and corporate governance from an ID perspective. Advice is also given on the appointment process, how best to present yourself and how to perform due diligence before accepting a position.

£975

https://www.pwc.co.uk/communities/documents/ned-programme/aspiring-ned-masterclass.pdf

E. NHS further reading resources

- Department of Health, for information about the latest policy initiatives

  https://www.gov.uk/government/organisations/department-of-health

- Care Quality Commission (CQC), which regulates all health and social care services in England

  https://www.cqc.org.uk/

- Healthcare Financial Management Association (HFMA), for information about NHS financial management

  https://www.hfma.org.uk

- NHS Providers is the membership organisation for the NHS hospital, mental health, community and ambulance services that treat patients and service users in the NHS

  https://nhsproviders.org

- Good Governance Institute

  https://www.good-governance.org.uk

Index

https://doi.org/10.1515/9783110706123-015